Also by Kate Fraser:

The Magic Handkerchief
(A tale for children)

Characters

Lili married to Fritz
Marta and Larry (their children)

Gabor: Lili's brother

Anyu and Apu: Lili's mother and father

Karin married to Peter
Vivien and Frederick (their children)

Vivien married to Paul
Karin and Peter (their children named for Vivien's
parents)

DO YOU REALLY WANT TO KNOW?

A Story of Survival and Redemption

KATE FRASER

Do You Really Want to Know? is a work of fiction based on historical documents from the 1930s and 40s blended with actual happenings which members of my family experienced during that period—and afterwards. While many of the described events are real, interpretations are my own and should be read as such.

This book is dedicated to my parents who left us
with an incredibly rich heritage
And to my children and grandchildren
Who I hope will always
Want to know

Elmsburg, New York 1962

Marta shoved her journal under her mattress. Time to get ready for school.

Austrian Alps 1945

Crack.

Just one. The thunder passed, waiting to make a more dramatic re-entrance. The birds resumed their warbling.

Lili shuddered at the defenseless violence and wrapped the thin gray overcoat tightly around her body, trembling in the frigid air. A patch of slimy mud threatened to pull the oversized boots right off her aching feet even as the stiff leather rubbed blisters on her sprained ankle.

Where was their guide? That young boy disappeared and reappeared like magic on the winding, mountain trail, oblivious to the tattered group attempting to follow him. All of them were out of her view. Fritz circled back to her, encouraging her to keep moving, but she could see the exhaustion etching his face. Occasional glimpses of colossal peaks capped with snow, emphasized the daunting task that was still ahead of them.

Booms of that lone gunshot from hours earlier kept echoing in Lili's mind while images of the bloody, motionless body competed with the alpine beauty surrounding her now.

She paused, catching her breath, straining to hear the people ahead of them. Silence. Until a sharp sound broke through. "Fritz." She grabbed his sleeve. "What was that?"

He stopped, concentrating. Panic flooded his face. "It's a dog."

A sound even more frightening than a gunshot. Guns didn't have noses to hunt down their prey. Dogs did.

The birds' constant chirping faded. The darkening clouds heralded rain. The dog's barking moved closer.

Was this the end?

ONE

Europe 1937

Vienna, Austria

Fritz

Could that be the alarm already? Fritz threw off the down comforter and rolled over to silence the jarring noise. The bedside lamp was on, and he was still dressed in yesterday's clothes. He had fallen asleep reading again, a frequent event for the 14 year-old bookworm. Sloshing cold water on his face, he smoothed down his hair's brown waves, brushed his teeth, and changed into a clean school uniform, wincing as he fastened the top button of his over-starched white shirt. He belted the flannel gray trousers, thankful that the childhood days of required shorts had passed. Knotting the navy tie, he headed to the kitchen. Maybe there was still some *stöllen* that delicious fruit bread coated with powdered sugar, left from last night's dessert. If his mother wasn't around, he could grab some on his way to school before Mutti noticed he had skipped breakfast.

Knapsack on his back and *stöllen* in his hand, Fritz exited the third floor of the elegant apartment in the *Liechtensteinstrasse* district. Afraid of missing the streetcar, he hurried down the narrow street framed by beige or yellow, three and four-storied buildings, ornate archways decorated with statues or engravings, all centuries old.

But according to the time on his new birthday watch, the streetcar was running late. Fritz groaned at the thought of missing his first class of German Literature. It was his favorite course and the only time he sat next to Gerti, his current love interest. All his friends thought she was attractive and stylish, but it was Fritz alone who could flirt while engaging her in conversation about poetry or Thomas Mann, subjects they were both passionate about. After a few minutes the streetcar arrived.

When it stopped at the curb in front of the school, Fritz sprinted, making it to class just in time. Gerti beamed, and his heartbeat accelerated. The teacher frowned at his undignified entrance and then began the lecture.

Fritz took out his notebook and started scribbling notes to convince both the teacher and Gerti that he was paying close attention. He was an admirable student and enjoyed learning. The time he spent voraciously reading at home made these first period presentations stimulating and prepared him to participate in the frequent discussions led by his teacher.

Besides literature, history also intrigued him. Unlike others his age, he focused on the snippets of information he saw on the newspaper headlines or overheard from adults and the radio. Remarkable events were occurring each day. The German airship Hindenburg had burst into flames in New Jersey. Hitler, the Fuehrer of Germany, was conspiring with segments of the Austrian government, planning the unification of the two countries. Targeting Jews as "the enemy" appeared to be a method for his achieving power. The first concentration camp at Buchenwald opened for political prisoners. The world seemed on the verge of upheaval.

At home there were whispered conversations that ended as soon as he walked into the room. Whether they were discussing current events or their family's precarious financial situation, he didn't know. His parents sheltered their only child from all unpleasantness, and that was just fine with him. The evil in the world couldn't touch him; it was just intellectual entertainment. His life was adventure waiting to happen.

*****

After school Fritz headed to the Boy Scout meeting as he did every Tuesday. Walking to the church basement around the corner, he beamed, anticipating today's meeting when they would make supply lists for a short campout in a few weeks.

Being a Scout was a liberating experience for him. Until his involvement with the Scouts, Fritz had been strictly a city boy, not even visiting relatives outside the metropolis of Vienna. But after the first exhilarating expedition to the Tyrolean Alps, he was hooked. The Scouts built their own shelters, dug latrines, cooked over campfires, hiked mountain trails, and swam in pristine alpine lakes. It often took weeks after such adventures to readjust from the freedom he felt in the mountains with his friends to the confines of city life and over-attentive parents.

Budapest, Hungary

Lili

Lili shifted the rucksack strap to her other shoulder,

avoiding her long black braid. She must be carrying ten kilograms of books, enough homework to extinguish her afternoon plans to go roller skating with her friend, Greta. The continual academic requirements of this ninth year of school still surprised Lili.

She stepped onto the narrow sidewalk of the cobbled streets built centuries ago for horse and carriage which wound around small grassy parks, punctuated with benches and fountains. Lili nodded to the grumpy neighbor walking his black poodle and circled around the young boys, intent on their sidewalk marble game.

As she entered the second floor of the five-story stucco apartment, she detected the tantalizing odor of fresh strudel. Helen, her governess, must still be working, and she specialized in delectable baked items. Now that Helen wasn't needed to supervise Lili and her brother anymore, she worked fewer hours – which meant less baking and cooking, so this was a welcomed treat.

"Smells incredible!" Lili called to Helen in the kitchen on the way to her bedroom. After shedding the white blouse and black skirt of her school uniform for a more comfortable soft knit dress, Lili headed back to the kitchen. Warm, crisp apple strudel with hot cocoa should help her homework be more palatable.

Her brother, Gabor, had gotten home first and beaten her to the rectangular wooden table in the corner of the small, tidy kitchen. He was already gobbling down a large portion of the pastry, cooked apples leaking out the side of his mouth. He grinned at her while shoveling in another mouthful, "*Hallo schätze*, I left you a bite."

Lili poked his ribs, beaming at being called his sweetheart. She adored her big brother even though he was a constant tease and had the appetite of a horse. Four years older and half a meter taller, Gabor, her only sibling, was the most important and stable person in her life. Governesses came and went with frequent regularity, but she could always count on her brother.

Their parents, *Anyu* and *Apu,* worked long hours at the downtown dry goods shop they owned with her aunt and uncle. Like today, they weren't around until the evening meal. They came home exhausted with few words or little affection available for their teenage children. Their parents' indifference offered Lili and Gabor more freedom than most of their peers. Because of their continual absence, Gabor and Lili didn't have to ask permission for outings or report on their whereabouts.

Lili was too much of a bookworm and a rule-follower to take advantage of their inattention, but Gabor relished the challenge of sneaking out at all hours, even while his parents were reading in the living room, for various escapades with his friends.

"Sandor and I are going to play some *füssball* in the park. Want to come?" Gabor asked.

"Too much homework," Lili groused, scowling. Sandor was her favorite of Gabor's many friends. His intense blue eyes often focused right at her, and sometimes he took the time to talk to her about books and, best of all, listened to her responses.

"I suppose you need to keep working hard if you are going to be a famous doctor like Uncle Miklos," he teased.

Lili's face lit up. She and Gabor both knew how rare women doctors were in Hungary. And she was passionate about this goal.

But then reality won her attention, a sigh extinguishing the enthusiasm. She pulled out her notebook while Gabor headed out the door. At times she wished she was more like her carefree brother. For Lili, everything was very serious – schoolwork and just … life. As she copied down math equations, she remembered the quote from Thomas Mann that they discussed in history class. She wanted to record it in her journal before she forgot because it seemed relevant to this present time in Europe. "Tolerance becomes a crime when applied to evil."

Upstairs In her bedroom she pulled open the top dresser drawer to fetch the flowered diary. It wasn't there. Rummaging around, she finally found it under her socks instead of beneath her underwear where it belonged. The leather bookmark had fallen out. Who could have read it? Gabor would have no interest. Helen couldn't even read Hungarian. She opened to her last entry several days ago. In her careful script, she saw the paragraphs pouring out her latest frustrations with *Anyu*. Her mother's distance and lack of emotional affection sometimes overwhelmed Lili with feelings of hurt and rejection. Lili now recoiled as she read her overdramatic words, "I just wish she were dead." Of course she didn't mean that. Was her mother the one who read this? And why?

During their *goulash* dinner of tender beef, onions, and carrots flavored with paprika, Gabor and *Apu* kept up a steady chatter about the events around them. In Russia, Josef Stalin continued his purge of Red Army generals. Hitler revealed more of his war plans during the Hassbach conference. Hungary, only an independent nation for 18 years, watched and waited. Gabor was fascinated by the drama around them, and usually Lili listened with some interest. But at the moment, none of it seemed relevant to her.

She lingered in the kitchen after dinner, watching her mother sip her steaming coffee. If she didn't do this now, she would lose her courage. Lili took a deep breath. "*Anyu*, did you read my journal?" Her mother looked startled. Setting the coffee cup back on the saucer, she pinched her lips, guilt shading her face.

To Lili's great surprise, tears slipped down *Anyu's* cheeks. Never had Lili seen her stoic mother cry, not even last year when her own father had died suddenly of a heart attack. "*Anyu*, I didn't mean what I wrote about you. I was just upset."

Anyu's tears turned into a torrent, her quivering chin shaking her words. "I am so sorry I haven't been a better mother. We never talk. You'll never tell me anything. That's why I wanted to read your journal, just to know what you think about and what is going on in your life. When I was your age, I could never talk to my mother… I'm worried the same thing is happening with us." She directed her pained stare at Lili. "What should I do? I have no idea how to even start being a decent mother."

Lili had no idea either.

She let her mother draw her into a stiff, awkward hug, hoping maybe they could figure it out together.

Berlin, Germany

Vivien

The rosy-cheeked toddler never stopped. Her mother, Karin Schmidt, put down the mending and again plucked her adventurous daughter from the edge of the staircase. A pile of wooden blocks caught Vivien's attention for a moment, but Karin knew the only way to keep that focus would be if she built precarious towers for Vivien to knock down. Each time the blocks would crash, Vivien giggled in delight. With a groan, Karin lowered herself to the floor, aware of her growing belly and the active baby kicking in her womb. These days alone with her daughter were so long. Karin missed the support of her family and friends in Munich, 584 kilometers away. Adult company was rare and limited to occasional excursions to the nearby park. During the two years they had been stationed here, most of her military acquaintances had relocated.

By the time her husband, Peter, got home, all he wanted to do was eat and sleep. Peter was an officer in the Wehrmacht, the Nazi regime's armed force and the heart of Germany's politico-military power. As he previously explained to her, its purpose was to regain lost territory as well as to gain new territory and dominate its neighbors. As the war effort continued to escalate, so did the time requirements and pressure on him. When he was home, stress always lined his face, and his focus seemed elsewhere. Although he attempted to be cheerful around his wife and young daughter, Karin resented his preoccupation with the military details which he no longer discussed with her.

As a result, Karin didn't know much about the current war. She and Peter rarely talked about anything concerning it. Some of her acquaintances had complained about shortages in stores, but she hadn't noticed any of that yet. They didn't have a radio or buy newspapers. Because Peter had decided travelling was getting dangerous, they had canceled their Christmas trip to see both their families in Munich. That disappointment was real and still stung her heart. Being seven months pregnant and chasing after fourteen-month-old Vivien took up most of her mental and physical energy. But loneliness prevailed.

She missed Peter's physical presence, but even more so, his friendship. During the early years of their marriage, they communicated their thoughts about everything. Now she couldn't remember the last time they had a deep conversation or shared a laugh.

Smash! The tumble of blocks interrupted Karin's

discontented thoughts and brought her back to the present. Vivien had found her favorite orange block and pounded it on the vanquished tower. Karin sighed. It was almost naptime. Vivien climbed onto her shrinking lap with an exuberant hug. Karin squeezed her back. Perspective restored. For now.

TWO

Elmsburg, New York 1963

Marta

It just wasn't going to work. Marta flung the hairbrush onto the floor. There was no way her brown, curly hair would look anywhere close to fashionable. As if that would help her fit in at Elmsburg High School. She must be the only flat-chested 14-year-old in all of Westchester County. She was sure no one in the entire school had parents who spoke German (or worse yet, Hungarian) at home. Her mother couldn't help her pick out cute clothes at Macy's or Alexander's because she had no concept of what was fashionable. Marta couldn't even claim an ordinary American name like Linda, Donna or Marlene. And then there was the most shameful secret that set her apart: her great aunt had numbers tattooed on her forearm that she refused to talk about.

Marta switched off the transistor radio. "It's my party, and I'll cry if I want to…" The week's top song echoed in her head.

The front door slammed, followed by chortles of boyish laughter. Larry didn't have trouble fitting in. He could hurl a baseball, slam homeruns, and friends always surrounded him. In some freakish genetic throwback, he even had blond hair and freckles. No one would ever call her younger brother Jew-boy or sissy.

Glancing at the clock, she realized the time for messing with her appearance was over. The school bus was due in a few minutes. Running downstairs, she grabbed her book satchel and lunch box, joining her brother's gang at the curb of the identical red brick, white-shuttered house next door.

As she climbed on the bus, Marta exhaled in relief when she noticed two empty seats. She could save one for Peggy her best, and only friend, who boarded last, giving them a chance to chatter for the last five minutes of the trip. They didn't have any classes together, and sometimes the lunchroom was too crowded for a decent conversation.

At the next stop, Peggy hurried onto the bus and stumbled over gym shoes and a lunch box in the aisle, plopping on the seat next to Marta. Her chubby face was sweaty but grinning. "I had to run for the bus stop. Stupid George hid my shoes again – this time un-der my parents' bed!" George was Peggy's dog, a dig-nified looking, but naughty collie. Marta chuckled, and Peggy joined in. After a few comments on their evening activities, the bus pulled up to the sprawling brick schoolhouse as the janitor was raising the Amer-ican flag on the pole.

Marta's first class was Math. She loved Math – and she was good at it. This was a mixed blessing. Because of the alphabetical seating chart, Billy Mahoney sat right behind her—the Billy Mahoney, star quarterback, charming and handsome, who just happened to be horrible at Math. Every day he welcomed her help, flashing his dimpled grin at her answers. However (or maybe because of that) many of the girls in class gave her disapproving glances, sometimes even whisper-ing the dreaded slur, "square." She recognized their jealousy, but that didn't soften the insult. It just heightened her awareness that she didn't belong. Not anywhere.

Today's class was spent on a review quiz. Even though it nagged at Marta's conscience, she placed her paper on the right side of the desk, so Billy could see it. His whispered, "Thanks," at the end of class red-dened her cheeks and warmed her heart.

Next came English. Marta's grades weren't quite as outstanding here, but she enjoyed the young, perky teacher, Mrs. Harris. As Marta slid into her seat, her eyes focused on the fancy calligraphy on the board: Understand yourself by understanding your family. Marta's stomach fluttered. What was this all about?

After the class settled into their seats, Mrs. Harris explained the assignment. Her voice sounded, to Marta, even more earnest than usual. "This is your major project for the semester. Each of you will learn about your family's heritage and share it with your classmates. Since you are learning about World War II in History class, you will be combining this into a related project with your History teacher." Marta heard some grumbling around her, but most of the surrounding faces seemed entranced.

"How do we find out all this stuff?" a girl in the second row blurted out. Mrs. Harris smiled, "You ask your parents and grandparents questions. I will give you a sheet with some ideas, but I think once you get started, it will be enjoyable."

Marta rolled her eyes, pressing her lips into a fine line. Enjoyable? Pulling things from her parents? And then worst of all – having to share with her classmates? As if she needed any more reasons to feel different.

Her face must have given her feelings away because as Mrs. Harris passed out the papers, she leaned over Marta's desk and whispered, "You are such an excellent writer; this will be easy for you."

Marta suppressed her sigh. She did have confidence in her writing ability, but she knew so little about her parents' early life in Budapest and Vienna. They never volunteered any information and changed the subject or left the room if her grandparents mentioned old memories. And every discussion Marta and her mother had about anything nowadays ended in an argument or a hostile stalemate.

Marta thrust the sheet of questions into the back of her notebook and shoved down all the concerns in her mind. The past was a long way from the present; too bad they couldn't remain separate.

Lili

Marta's mother, Lili, rinsed off her lunch plate and placed it in the dishwasher. She still couldn't believe this noisy contraption washed dishes better than she could. After wiping off the counters and sweeping the floors, she carried her cup of coffee to the living room. The house was spotless. The ham and potato casserole for dinner was ready to go in the oven. She had three hours before school was out and the children were home. And to be honest with herself, she was bored.

This was not the life she had envisioned for herself as a young teenager in Budapest, Hungary. She had hoped for marriage and children someday, but back then her burning passion was to become a doctor.

Ever since her toddler days, Lili was fascinated by injuries and even by blood. As a young girl, she bandaged her dolls, her stuffed animals, and Struppi, the family poodle. Her uncle Miklos, a doctor in neighboring Gyor, would give her his old medical magazines and answer her myriad of questions. She treasured her tenth birthday gift of a real first-aid kit which came in handy for her adventurous brother Gabor's cuts and scrapes.

And now—she had a beautiful two-story house, surrounded by a manicured lawn and trimmed shrubbery, in the suburbs of New York City. She had a hardworking husband, Fritz, and two darling children, Marta and Larry, and a black Scottish terrier, Scotty. They were all healthy and safe. There was plenty of opportunity and freedom available in the United States. No dangers threatened their lives. Although she was grateful for all of that, as time went on, Lili realized how empty and insignificant she felt. Even invisible sometimes.

Her neighbors were pleasant enough, but she was never invited to their coffee klatches, their Mahjong games, or their country club events. Even if she had been invited, she had no interest in going. They all seemed so thoroughly American while she still had trouble with the language, couldn't stomach corndogs or Cokes, and had no desire for the latest hair styles or fashions. How she longed to have an intelligent conversation or some meaningful activities and involvement outside of their house's four walls. But she didn't know where to start.

Things were better when they lived in the Bronx even though the apartment was tiny. The playground had been a wonderful place to meet neighborhood women, many of whom were also recent immigrants from Europe. She had helped organize a co-op nursery school and took a few night classes at the local college, thinking that becoming a teacher would be more achievable now than her earlier dreams of becoming a doctor. But Fritz wanted better schools for the children, and successful men were moving their families to the surrounding suburbs. So here they were, twenty miles away from the Bronx, pursuing the American Dream in Elmsburg, New York.

Fritz appeared happy. His job overseeing a garment factory in Manhattan was demanding but according to him, satisfying. When home, he loved caring for the yard, nurturing each rose bush that lined the driveway.

Larry and his many neighborhood friends spent their free hours riding bikes on the surrounding streets or playing baseball in an empty lot. He came home to eat or sleep and never caused any trouble.

Then there was Marta. Lili frowned. She had always been concerned about Marta. Even as a baby, she was easily irritated and pushed away Lili's affection. She didn't seem to connect well with others, and her smiles were infrequent. Books were her main companions. Since she had become a teenager, all those behaviors intensified. Lili found herself tiptoeing around her daughter trying not to ignite another explosion. Their conversations were few and seemed stuck on the superficial level. Unfortunately, their relationship reminded her of the relationship with her own mother when she was Marta's age. Until it all changed.

Vivien Harris

Vivien eyed the tremendous stack of papers in the center of her desk. Being an English teacher was a dream come true, but correcting five class-loads of writing assignments created a full-time job in itself. She smiled ruefully, remembering the veteran English teacher's advice to keep her life simple and just focus on assigning grammar worksheets.

However, these writing papers, no matter what the topic, gave her a window into her students' souls. Finding the time to read and correct them and still pursue her role as a newlywed was a continual challenge, but gratifying.

Vivien still found it hard to believe she now was married, and to someone like Paul, who as the cliché said, surpassed her wildest dreams. She didn't consider herself attractive, witty, or fascinating, and yet Paul was all this and more—tall, dark, and yes, handsome, in addition to considerate and compassionate. He knew his own mind and had a deep, quiet strength. They had met a few years ago in a children's literature class for educators at New York University. It was Vivien's favorite class by far. She loved to read, and many of the assigned children's books were new to her. She devoured them like freshly baked bread, balm to her lonely soul. Because numbers were his thing, Paul didn't share that passion, and his frustration became obvious to her and to their instructor. This perceptive professor paired them together for the final project – and the rest was history. Not only did they fall in love, but Paul's family welcomed her with open arms. And the project earned Vivien and Paul an A+!

Now her life with Paul and as a teacher buried her past in welcome layers of distraction and even contentment.

Noticing the time, she thrust the writing papers into her briefcase. Paul taught Math at the high school two towns over, and he would be here soon to pick her up. His briefcase would be almost empty.

As she erased the board, she remembered that unobtrusive girl from second period, Marta, and her distinct reaction to the family history assignment. She had looked panicked. Vivien understood. She wondered again just why she was assigning this particular topic.

History Project

Marta trudged up the three concrete steps and pushed open the white front door, dropping her satchel in the foyer. It landed on the floor with a loud thud: plenty of homework.

Her mom met her in front of the kitchen with a cheery grin and a soft kiss on the top of her head, "Good day at school?"

"Yeah, I guess," Marta muttered. How was she ever going to do that stupid English assignment?

On most days she took her after-school snack to the privacy of her room. Today, determined to start interviewing her mom before Larry or her dad got home, she placed her notebook and sharpened pencil on the kitchen table and grabbed a small bag of chips.

She exhaled, focusing on her snack. "We are supposed to learn all about our family history for English class. It will be combined with a History project. I have a list of questions to ask you." Her mumbled words tumbled together. She peered up at her mother through her overgrown bangs.

Her mother stiffened, perching on the corner of a kitchen chair. She seemed as awkward as Marta in this unknown territory, yet she pasted on her ever-ready smile.

"What was your life like when you were my age?" Marta began.

"Well, when I was 14, my life was pretty ordinary. We had a beautiful apartment near the center of Budapest. My parents spent most of the day in their dry goods store downtown. I had a series of governesses who took care of me when I was younger and helped the other servant with cooking and cleaning. I adored my older brother, Gabor, who sometimes let me tag along with him and his friends. I was a decent student at our gymnasium which is equivalent to an American high school. Science classes fascinated me, and I dreamed of being a doctor," Lili paused, noticing the astonished expression on her daughter's face.

"You've never told me you wanted to be a doctor," Marta said with suspicion. "And how come we never see Uncle Gabor if you two were so close?"

"Australia is a long way away. He did visit here once when you were a baby. And I guess my dreams changed. Instead of a doctor, I am now a blessed wife and mother." She eyed Marta, trying to persuade them both about this statement.

Marta frowned, trying to adjust to this new information. "Linda's mother is a doctor. People can be both."

"Yes, Marta, they can," her mother continued, "but when I was 14 my life changed drastically."

Marta's stomach dropped. Here came the hard stuff, the real elephant in the room. She pressed the pencil down so hard, the point snapped. "How did it change?"

A cheerful shout from the foyer interrupted the conversation. "Hey, I'm home." Larry bounded up the stairs to the kitchen. "I'm starving!" he announced as he did every day.

Lili rose from the table, hugged her son, and poured him a glass of milk while he fetched a bowl of cereal. Larry's cheeks were rosy, his blond hair disheveled, and he smelled like fresh grass and sunshine. He was a welcome distraction for her.

Marta picked up her notebook and headed upstairs with a sigh of relief. And questions swirling.

Who Am I?

Later that evening she and Fritz relaxed in their leather living room chairs, skimming through the many pages of the New York Times. Dinnertime conversation had been dominated by Larry and Fritz reviewing each play of the Yankees' last baseball game. Marta was silent as usual, but tonight that quietness rankled Lili. How much did Marta really want to know? How much did Lili really want to tell her?

Fritz laid down the editorial section and gazed at his wife. "How was your day, dear?" Lili sifted through her mind for the little tidbits she tried to store up each day to convince Fritz (and herself) that her life in Elmsburg was interesting and fulfilling.

"When I was walking Scotty around the neighborhood this morning, the Katz's bulldog charged at us with his fierce growl. Patricia came right out to put his leash on. We chatted for a few minutes. She thinks I should join the PTA and help with their spring auction."

Lili glanced at Fritz to see if he was still paying attention. Her hands were sweaty. "I'm almost finished reading The Keepers of the House. It's so engrossing. Today I got a letter from Gabor telling me about their vacation in New Zealand. I sure wished they lived closer. Oh, and Marta has a family research project to do for English class. She already started asking me questions."

Fritz's eyebrows arched in surprise. He knew about the communication difficulties between his wife and his daughter. "Yes?" he prompted, not sure if he did want to hear more.

Lili glanced at the clock, refolded the newspaper section, and jumped to her feet, "I'd better tuck the children into bed." She paused before climbing the stairs. Why was she avoiding sharing anything more with Fritz? He seemed interested in pursuing the conversation. Marta's research project must be a more fascinating topic than the interaction of neighborhood dogs.

Larry was sitting in bed, leafing through the latest issue of "Sports Illustrated." Lili adjusted his covers. "Good night, son." He dropped the magazine and threw his arms around her, still an affectionate youngster at age ten.

"Night, Mom," he answered as she turned out the light and closed the door.

"Love you," they both chorused.

Marta was hunched over her desk, glaring at her Science homework. Lili knew this was her least favorite subject, but she had stopped offering help after too many snappish exchanges. "Almost done, sweetheart?" Lili asked, hesitating in the doorway.

"Just about," Marta answered. "I'll turn out the light when I finish. And Mom?" Lili turned from the doorway to face her daughter. "Maybe we can work on those questions again tomorrow."

They locked eyes for a moment, and Lili felt a glimmer of something akin to hope, mixed with the already present apprehension. Could she and Marta actually have a real conversation? Where would that conversation lead?

Fritz

Fritz rubbed his eyes and attempted to smooth out the wrinkles on his brow. He sagged deeper into his chair.

It had been a longer day than usual with an intense staff meeting about the threatened union strike and an hour delay on the commuter train. He entertained the thought of joining his wife upstairs for the evening routines but decided against it. Maybe this was the opportunity for a breakthrough with Lili and Marta. He knew how hard an adjustment it had been for Lili to move from the Bronx to suburbia. He didn't care for their success-driven neighbors any more than she did but had little contact with them. He was grateful for a job he enjoyed most of the time and for co-workers from a similar background who could also participate in intelligent conversations. Lili used to enjoy the deep discussions in her previous college classes. Maybe it would be a good idea for her to take a few courses again, get out of the house, and pursue some of her old goals.

Fritz felt a kinship with Marta. Her introspective and sometimes dark moods reminded him of his younger self, although he had been much more outgoing and social. Marta was generous in showing Fritz affection and didn't respond with sharpness to him like she often did to her mom. He wished she would appreciate the privileged life she had been given, but then again, he hadn't when he was Marta's age either.

Larry was more of a puzzle. Fritz did not understand, or even like baseball, but was willing to try, so he could have some common ground with his son. Larry bounced with action and adrenalin. His pleasant even-temperedness balanced his sister's erratic moods.

What was Fritz to make of that very abrupt reference to a family research project? He had made peace with his past. The thought of unearthing all the details and presenting them to his daughter troubled him. He took some deep breaths and tried to swallow the knots of anxiety in his stomach.

Different Like Me

The next morning Marta awoke with the shadow of a dream dancing around inside her head. She hated when that happened. It was like trying to touch a snowflake, the elusiveness disappearing at her fingertips. Somehow that short conversation with her mom must have unlocked unfamiliar thoughts.

Marta was so distracted as she prepared for school that she didn't realize her blouse and skirt clashed until the bus pulled up to the curb. Plaid and flowers. Great. More ammunition for the cool group.

Math class was always a balm to her soul. Numbers behaved with so much rationality! Billy asked her questions twice and thanked her with that dimpled grin.

As she entered the English room, she noticed the

same words on the blackboard, with a few added flourishes. After the bell rang, Mrs. Harris stood and asked, "Who found out something interesting about their family's history last night?" With amazement Marta saw almost every hand shoot up. Mrs. Harris raised her eyebrows in surprise.

She called on Tom first. "I knew my dad fought on the frontlines in France, but I never knew he faked his age and was an American soldier at 15." Others nodded in agreement.

"How many of you had fathers or grandfathers that served our country during World War II?" Mrs. Harris asked. Again almost every student raised their hand.

Mary jumped right in, "My mother worked for the Red Cross making care packages to send to soldiers. She lived in a boarding house in Boston and worked twelve hours a day."

Cheryl blurted out, "My uncle flew helicopters for the Army."

"My grandma was a military nurse in France," Bob said. "She almost got killed there when she was on the front lines."

Marta was flabbergasted. How did they know all this? And here was more confirmation. No one else had a background like hers.

Mrs. Harris reminded the class to write down what they were learning about their families and to be sure to look at all the questions on the sheet.

Sam, who was even more of a square than Marta, raised his hand, "My family has already traced our genealogy. My ancestors came here on the Mayflower, and I am related to King Henry VI." The class turned to stare at him, impressed.

Eyeing the clock, Mrs. Harris shifted their attention to analyzing the next chapter of Hungary.

As the bell rang, Marta tried to beat the rush of students to the door. Her face must have broadcast her nervousness because Mrs. Harris intercepted her. "You looked uncomfortable today. Is there something wrong?"

Marta felt tears threatening to escape but with a determined effort held them back, clearing her throat, "I am so different from everyone else, and so is everyone in my family. I don't even want to talk about all this heritage stuff in class."

Mrs. Harris patted her shoulder. "Yes, but these differences are essential. The United States is a melting pot of many diverse types of people. And just so you know, you are not the only person in this class that has a unique family and story."

"I'm not?" Marta chewed her lip.

"Someday we will have a long, private conversation about that," Mrs. Harris said with a gentle sigh.

The late bell rang, and Marta gave her teacher a confused smile before she hurried off to her next class.

Vivien Harris watched her go down the hall and wondered, again, what she was getting herself into.

Understood

As she climbed into Paul's Camaro, Vivien leaned over for a brief kiss. They filled the 20-minute commute home on the Taconic Parkway with vignettes from their day's classes. Each of them had favorite characters to report on. Laughing together about the outlandish things teenagers said and did was always a satisfying transition time.

"Lots of correcting?" Paul asked.

"Of course," Vivien exhaled.

"Well then, I volunteer to be tonight's chef." Paul squeezed Vivien's hand.

Later, over fried pork chops, apple sauce, and roasted potatoes, Vivien told him about the new family project she had assigned and about Marta's reaction. Marta wasn't one of their usual "characters." In fact Vivien hadn't noticed her much all year. She knew why she was so focused on her now. Slivers from her past threatened to emerge.

Paul gazed at her with compassionate perception. "Are you planning on sharing your family's story as well?"

Vivien hesitated. "I'm not sure. I don't have to, and I don't want to, but somehow it seems wrong for me to withhold my story when I expect my students to share theirs."

Her husband cupped her trembling fingers. "Who your parents were and what they did does not define you. I claim you now, and my family does as well. We have become your forever family."

Leaning her head on his strong shoulder, Vivien nodded. "I wonder why I'm asking my students to do something that I am not willing to do myself."

A loud crash interrupted them. Snuggles, their orange tabby cat, had nosed the serving platter to the floor. After the cleanup, a chatty phone call from Paul's mom, and other evening routines, the discussion seemed forgotten. Yet it swirled around in Vivien's mind as she corrected papers and it intertwined her dreams throughout the night.

After School

The school bus would arrive in 15 minutes. Larry had a Cub Scout meeting after school, so Lili set out a fresh plate of Marta's favorite brownies which filled the air with a rich chocolaty smell. She tightened the resolve she had been struggling with all day. Lili was ready to delve into her past with Marta. Her daughter had a right to fill in all the missing pieces. This was her family's history. The heritage they shared.

She wished Fritz would agree and join with her in

this. However, that didn't seem to be his intention. Was she prepared to relive it all? Was Marta mature enough to handle the whole story? Lili didn't know the answers to either question. Maybe she was about to find out.

As Marta climbed on the school bus, she remembered Peggy had a doctor's appointment that afternoon. Just as well because she didn't feel like talking to anyone. School had been awful. During third period "mean Mary" had noticed her mismatched outfit and spread the word to her gang. By lunchtime, there were plenty of sly glances aimed her way. She spent the day trying to be as invisible as possible, spending study hall in the Band practice room reviewing her clarinet parts. Why did she care so much about what other people thought? Especially stupid people.

Was she ready to hear what her mother had to say? And once she had all that information, was she ready to share it with her English class?

THREE

Europe 1938 - 1942

Changes

Vienna 1938

Everything had changed overnight. As Fritz sprinted to catch the streetcar for school on this Monday in March, the evidence surrounded him on every side. Nazi flags and banners, brandishing anti-Jewish slogans, swastikas, and pictures of Hitler decorated the quaint architecture. Standing in the crowded streetcar, he observed Nazi party buttons on numerous lapels. Bold, black newspaper headlines announced the new German Anschluss. His thoughts swirled. The anticipated and feared union of Austria with Germany had arrived.

Being Jewish had never been an issue in Fritz's life. His family didn't go to the synagogue or practice any Jewish rituals. Generations as far back as he knew, ignored religion. They were respected and accepted by the entire community around them, Christians and Jews. His father was a decorated lieutenant in World War One. They even had a Christmas tree and painted Easter eggs as did many other secular European Jews.

But all of a sudden it appeared being Jewish was an issue. A big issue. Fritz felt nervous. And scared.

That day, and the ones following, passed in a frenzied blur. Fritz watched as Jewish-looking pedestrians were arrested at random by Nazi soldiers. Elderly Jews were forced to scrub the pavement on their knees. Students were heckled at school and anywhere else. He observed, pretending not to see, as bullies pushed two boys' faces into their lunch. Thankful for his Aryan features, he kept reminding himself, "Just stay invisible."

Abounding rumors circulated among his classmates. Radio and newspapers reported that Leftists and Jewish intellectuals were being detained or disappeared to somewhere in a concentration camp system.

Confusion, fear, and hopelessness spread and intensified exponentially among all the Jews, regardless of their social, religious, or professional status. Fritz felt it among his friends and even his reticent family.

And things kept escalating each day. Some people attempted to relocate although options were disappearing. All Jewish passports were invalidated. Permission to leave the country took great sums of money. Prominent Jewish citizens were even committing suicide.

What was the best reaction? Some of his classmates were eager to greet each other with the Nazi salute and spout the new dogma. Fritz tried to remain inconspicuous. He didn't feel Jewish. And with his light brown hair and stubby nose, he didn't look Jewish. How long could he keep up the pretense?

He found out the next day at school in the hall between classes. A loud group of boys pushed their way through the crowd. Hans, who was in his Science class noticed Fritz. "Hey, I think this guy is Jewish," he shouted to his cronies. "Pull his pants down. That'll prove it." Before Fritz could make an escape, the bullies gathered in a knot around him. One of them yanked his belt and trouser button open. Another shoved his pants down to his ankles. Then the late bell rang, and his tormenters fled. Fritz hurriedly rearranged his clothing and snuck out the school building, face crimson, humiliated to the core, trying to again blend in on his early commute home with his tears and shame stuffed inside.

But now the things he heard and read took on new meaning. Each day more regulations restricting the rights of Jews were announced on the radio or posted on buildings. By week's end, most public places were forbidden to Jews. Even park benches were segregated. Jewish businesses were transferred to non-Jews.

And then the announcement came that schools would be segregated. So on the next Monday morning all Jewish students, including Fritz, were removed from their Gentile classrooms. No time for goodbyes. His life was upended, along with the other two million Jews who resided in Vienna. He kept wondering how this all could be happening. The world was going crazy.

The following week in April, Fritz pushed his shoulders back, held his head erect, and strode the two blocks to his new school with all-Jewish classmates. These last few weeks had drained his passion for being in school, but having friends and keeping a semblance of normalcy drove him on. Starting over was daunting, but Fritz refused to give up. Numbly he moved through each day.

Tension dominated the evenings at home. More reports about Jewish deportation to concentration camps surfaced in worried conversations. His parents whispered their discussions in Hungarian which Fritz barely understood, but he perceived the anxiety, and the possible impending disasters. Then compounding all this came the news that most countries had closed their borders to Jewish refugees.

At dinner the next day, Fritz's father cleared his throat. "I have an announcement to make. We are moving to Gyor."

"What?" Fritz squealed before he could stop himself. He had heard vague conversations about Gyor, a small town outside of Budapest, Hungary. Why would anyone want to move there?

"It makes sense for us," his father continued. "The Nazis aren't occupying Hungary yet. I still have my Hungarian citizenship. Many of my relatives still live there. I am an honored World War I veteran. It will be a safe place for us."

Fritz clamped his lips together so his thoughts wouldn't escape through his mouth. It seemed like a horrible idea to him. More than horrible. Austrians looked down on Hungarians as barbarians; their culture and history was inferior to Austria's. The language was certainly barbaric. Everything dear to him was in Vienna. All his friends and experiences. His childhood memories.

As they prepared for the move, Fritz wanted to scream his anguish. He couldn't bring anything valuable out of the country, so even his books and stamp collection had to be sold. Fritz felt like he was in the middle of a dream that was happening to someone else. Not just a dream—a horrid nightmare.

Now an Outcast

Budapest 1940

Lili frowned, pursing her lips as she emerged from her apartment. The sunshine already promised a glorious morning on this November day, but something seemed different. She couldn't quite put her finger on what it was as she rushed to school, but she didn't want to think about it. Today was a special day, and nothing was going to spoil it! After weeks of preparation, she and Greta were presenting their science project along with the two most handsome boys in their whole class, Klaus and Janci. The four of them had spent many hours researching and creating an oral report and a detailed model of the human brain, showing how different styles of music affect learning. Last night Klaus had even walked her home after they were done working to celebrate their finished project with a treat of hazelnut ice cream from Levendula's Ice Cream Parlor.

As Lili entered the school building, she did notice one obvious difference. Next to the Hungarian flag that always greeted them in the entryway flew the dreaded Nazi banner. Inside, students gathered in small whispering groups instead of the usual boisterous clusters.

Science class was first period. Lili had a large satchel with her parts of the project. When she arrived in the classroom, she observed Greta, Klaus, and Janci clutching their bags also. As was customary, they stood when their teacher entered the room. But to Lili's surprise, Mr. Hadik raised his arm in the Nazi salute and even more shocking to her, most of the class returned the salute.

"Instead of starting with our science presentations," Mr. Hadik said in an even voice devoid of emotion. "I have an announcement from the headmaster." This was unusual. All the students seemed to be holding their breath in anticipation of what else could interrupt their normal routine. "As of this period, all Jewish pupils are to be dismissed from school."

Everyone looked stunned. After a few minutes of utter silence, Jacob Reimer timidly raised his hand. "Where are we to go, sir? And what about our science projects?" Jacob was the son of a prominent Jewish doctor and often Lili's rival for the top science grades.

"Your classmates will carry on your projects. Clear out your desks and take all school-issued items to the main office." Mr. Hadik directed a harsh squint at Jacob.

Lili's stomach flip-flopped. Could this be happening? To her? She passed her science bag to Greta who offered a sympathetic smile. Lili emptied the meager personal contents of her desk into her knapsack, holding on to her pile of textbooks. When she passed Klaus's desk, he refused to meet her eyes, looking straight ahead, lips pinched together.

Without a word, the small group of exiled Jewish students trudged down the hall, eyes downcast. Jacob sidled up next to her. Behind his horn-rimmed glasses, his brown eyes appeared ready to overflow.

"My project was better than yours anyway," Lili whispered to him. He proffered a slight grin which disappeared as they arrived at the office.

The headmaster stood in the doorway, arms crossed and mouth downturned, with a large carton beside him. "Put your books in the box. Tomorrow you will report to the Kolozsvar Jewish High School."

Lili pushed open the heavy, engraved wooden door. Outside the sun still shone in a bright blue sky, and the birds chirped in sweet harmony. Didn't they know her life had just been turned upside down? Would she ever see her friends or teachers again?

The new Nazi signs full of swastikas and anti-Jewish sentiments plastered on all the buildings that had eluded her awareness earlier, all of a sudden crowded her vision. Would everyone know she was Jewish now? What would happen to her and her family? She shuddered, imagining what could be around the corner.

Leaving Berlin

1940

Vivien shrieked as two-year-old Fredrik knocked down her wooden dollhouse again. Karin Schmidt sighed. Vivien had been an active toddler, but Fredrik was a tornado. Nothing appeared to delight him more than upsetting his older sister, destroying her toys, and hearing her scream.

Tonight's dinner was more complicated than usual – sauerbraten to celebrate Peter's birthday. The beef roast had marinated for days with wine, carrots, and lots of onions. The blended gravy simmered on the stove as Karin started boiling the dumplings. Cucumber salad with sweet vinaigrette sat on the counter.

Vivien's new doll diverted her attention, and Fredrik tossed dollhouse furniture throughout the parlor. So much for Karin's far-fetched plan of calm, rosy-cheeked cherubs awaiting their father.

The front door slammed, alerting Vivien and Fredrik to their papa's arrival. They tumbled on top of each other, rushing to greet him. "Happy Birthday!" Karin called from the kitchen. As she reached over the children to hug him, she noticed the grim set of his jaw and his veiled gray eyes. Something was wrong. "Dinner is almost ready," she continued with a nervous smile.

Peter gave the children a brief hug and then faced his wife, face cold and sober, fists clenched at his side. "We are moving to Budapest. Tomorrow. We need to eat now, so we can start packing."

Karin's thoughts whirled. Budapest? Some of her friends who were married to Nazi officers had already been transferred to places like Paris and Copenhagen, but Budapest? Tomorrow? She should have tried to read the newspaper more often. She hadn't even realized that Hungary was now allied with the Nazis. To be uprooted from Germany, the country of her birth and all her family and friends to such a destination as Budapest? Hungarian was probably the most unintelligible language in the world! And she could not recall ever hearing anything endearing about Hungary or Budapest.

Despite her churning stomach, dinner tasted delicious to Karin, but Peter didn't voice any appreciation. The children sensed the somber mood and didn't carry on with their usual demands and chatter. After they settled into bed, each one clutching their favorite teddy bear, Karin went downstairs, brain spinning and heart somersaulting to face her husband and their new, uncertain future.

Gyor Countryside

1940

Gray. The sky was dripping gray. The ancient stone buildings were a slimy gray. The people ambling along the gray cobbled streets looked gray. And Fritz's mood was gray. Here he was in the middle of summer, on another rainy day, stuck in this provincial town with nothing much to do but study his Hungarian textbook. The complicated pronunciations were a continual frustration. Like *Viszontlatasar*. All those letters just to say goodbye! At this rate, he would never be able to attend school here in Hungary or even find friends to communicate with.

Fritz slammed the book down on the rickety desk. Grabbing his rain slicker and cap, he stepped into the drizzle, pulling his bicycle from the shrubs behind the house. His bicycle! The one ticket to freedom and escape he had found in Gyor. With the money from selling his stamp collection in Vienna, Fritz's father bought him this sturdy, blue, one-speed, magical vehicle.

Pedaling with his pent-up energy, it didn't take Fritz long to reach the surrounding countryside. Brown-spotted cows and rolling green meadows added some color to the grayness. A few ribbons of bright sunlight even pushed through the overcast skies.

In the midst of his loneliness the freedom to explore was exhilarating. He spent his only hours of happiness investigating the rural landscape surrounding Gyor. Despite the large number of his father's relatives in the area, few had children his age, and only a few of them spoke some German. Except one family. Fritz's bike was automatically drawn to the road on which Clari lived.

Clari was a third, or maybe fourth cousin. She was pretty. No, she was beautiful! Her bold friendliness had attracted Fritz who enjoyed being flirtatious. And wonder of wonders – she spoke German and Hungarian and delighted in the idea of being his language tutor. Clari and his bicycle kept Fritz from sinking into total despair over everything he left behind in Vienna.

When he clanged the bicycle's bell, Clari came running out of the house. But today, her face matched the grayness Fritz had been trying to dodge.

"We are leaving," she blurted out. "Tomorrow. The owner of Papi's shop is a Nazi. He is no longer willing to rent to Papi, and we heard things are getting worse soon." Her face was ashen, lip trembling, so unlike her usual buoyant self. "Yellow stars, transports, all that stuff that's already been going on in Vienna."

Fritz was stunned. Clari was leaving. The Nazi craziness was following them here – to Gyor? "Where are you going?"

"We are arranging a walk." Her voice was hollow. He raised his eyebrows. "Through the mountains. To Switzerland."

They gazed at each other in silence. Fritz had heard rumors of escapes to Switzerland, and he was sure Clari had also. Competent guides must be found, paid with a lot of money, and trusted through treacherous conditions. All possessions were sold or left behind except for what could be carried in a knapsack.

"So, this is goodbye?" he ventured. In answer she grabbed his shoulders and planted a tender kiss on his lips. He responded with a fierce hug and a fervent kiss, tinged with sorrow. Another anchorless relationship.

From the doorway Clari's mother called her. Fritz waved at them both and rode off, returning into the grayness. Half a kilometer from home, his bike careened off the road. A flat tire. It figured. What else could go wrong?

Budapest 1942

Yellow Star

Before turning the corner to the grocery store, Lili searched the busier street ahead. Only the usual crawl of Friday shoppers, parcels in their arms, were visible on the sidewalk. If Lili shifted her basket at a certain angle, it hid the yellow star sewn onto the front of her coat. If she walked fast, she would be home before curfew. If she was fortunate, no soldiers would appear on her route.

Berzi's grocery store was bustling. Tables of colorful fruits and fresh vegetables outside invited the discerning shopper. Lili kept her eyes straight ahead, so she didn't have to encounter the all too familiar sign, "Jews Verboten." Further down the street, Stein's grocery store had no tables displaying produce outside. The yellow star in the window allowed Lili to enter although the meager selection of groceries inside was not welcoming, bare shelves predominating.

As she placed her few purchases from Stein's in her basket, she saw a somewhat familiar face.

"Hello, Lili!" Jacob Reimer's cheerful voice boomed.

Lili was startled. She almost hadn't recognized Jacob. He had grown so much taller, and his body and voice were now that of a man's. How long had it been? Those innocent school days of two years earlier seemed a lifetime ago. Jacob had never shown up at Kolozsvor High School which had closed after a few months anyway.

Jacob joined her on the street, offering to carry her basket along with his. They chattered about the small jobs and limited activities they had been involved in since school closed. Suddenly Jacob's face paled. Out of nowhere appeared two German soldiers, bodies at attention, eyes roving the crowd around them. There was no way to avoid them. No place to disappear.

"You there," one of them spat at Jacob. Lili could see Jacob's entire body trembling. "Papers," the taller soldier snarled. Jacob set down the baskets, pulling his papers from inside his coat. Lili produced hers also. The soldier glanced at hers, sneering, "Go home, kike. And stay off the streets." He kicked over the grocery baskets and turned all his attention to Jacob, "You, Jew-boy, come with us."

<h1 style="text-align:center">Budapest 1942</h1>

<h1 style="text-align:center">Schoolgirl</h1>

Karin Schmidt watched Vivien twirl in front of the mirror, swirling her plaid dress around her and tapping her shiny, new, black patent-leather shoes. Vivien was bubbling with anticipation for her very first day of school in kindergarten. Karin wished she could share this excitement with her daughter instead of worrying. *Does she know enough Hungarian? Would she miss us too much? Will the other children be kind to her?*

"Time for breakfast." Karin hugged her daughter. In the kitchen Peter and Fredrick were already at the table which was covered with a scrumptious spread of meats, cheeses, hard rolls, and even Vivien's favorite—poppy seed croissants.

"A time to celebrate," Peter beamed at his daughter. "You are now a student."

"I am a student too!" four- year- old Fredrick insisted. His family chuckled and started filling their plates. Peter impeccably dressed in his Nazi uniform, picked at his food, and then stood up, kissed the top of his children's heads, and hugged his wife goodbye.

Moments later, Karin, holding on to Vivien's and Fredrick's hands, set off down the crowded street. She was starting to appreciate, just a little bit, the beauty of the ornate stone buildings, but not enough to quell her continual longing for home, family, and friends—and the cultural ambience of Berlin.

They arrived at the school within a few blocks. The courtyard was already awash with boys and girls of all sizes in matching plaid uniforms. Vivien gripped her mother's hand. A stout, cheerful woman stood in the doorway of Vivien's classroom, greeting each child. Inside, Karin pried off her daughter's sweaty hand and guided her to an empty desk. The children surrounding her were chattering away in Hungarian, of course. Karin knew if she didn't leave right away, she would be the one crying.

Later that afternoon as Karin and Fredrick waited outside the school gates, she was amazed to see Vivien running with several other children, sporting a wide grin, braids disheveled, and face flushed. While the children found their families, Vivien joined in the goodbyes – in Hungarian! She proceeded to entertain her mother all the way home with the day's events and her new vocabulary.

Vivien's enthusiasm lasted throughout dinner-time although Peter was more distracted than usual. He wouldn't meet Karin's eyes or respond to Vivien's chatter. Karin tried to engage him in conversation, "I noticed the Cohen's apartment is empty. Do you know where they moved?" Peter changed the subject.

The next morning Karin observed that the two apartments on either side of them were also boarded up.

On Duty in Budapest

1942

Three staccato shots resonated like a snare drum in the shadowy, deserted street. Peter Schmidt tightened his grip on the cold, steel pistol, whitening his knuckles. He adjusted the black hat embellished with an eagle crest, showing his rank as an elite Gestapo officer. His stomach grumbled. Savory fragrances of cooking sausage, cabbage, and onions drifting from open windows reminded him it was dinner time. And now dinner would be delayed.

As he rounded the corner, Peter saw a crumpled figure, half on the sidewalk, half on the street. A stark, white foot extended from baggy gray trousers. A scuffed slipper sat in the gutter. The gray-haired head lay in a widening pool of crimson. The coppery smell of fresh blood and death already tainted the air.

The soldier waiting at the curb saluted Peter. "Heil Hitler"

Peter returned the salute. His curt nod demanded an explanation.

"This man wore a star, but he had no papers. He tried to run away."

Peter nodded again. He pushed his shiny black boot tip against the clump of rags, careful to avoid the sticky blood. The frail body turned over, revealing a wrinkled face and blue eyes – widened and blank in death. Blue eyes terribly familiar.

Peter's stomach lurched. He clenched his fist and fought back unaccustomed tears and overwhelming memories. Vacations on the Baltic Sea coast – the cheerful bantering of his siblings as they splashed in the water, the flaky tart apple strudel his grandmother always packed in abundance, and the special times he and his grandfather spent together rowing the dory. His grandfather always encouraging his youngest grandson with gentle words and his warm, lively, blue eyes.

"Get rid of it," Peter barked to the corporal, turning away. His hands still trembled as he holstered his pistol.

His day finished, his weary steps now plodded home, his posture still erect, tears still on his cheeks. His wife, Karin's, birthday dinner, *Sachertorte*, and two excited children awaited him.

And the memories of blue eyes.

FOUR

Elmsburg, New York 1963

My Story

Lili heard the front door open. She switched off the classical radio station in the middle of her favorite Mozart Piano Nocturne, pasting on the customary, cheery smile which covered her habitual inner turmoil. The effort was worthless, for Marta entered engulfed in her own gray storm cloud, projecting her emotions for all to see.

"Bad day?" Lili murmured. Marta slammed her satchel down.

"Just the normal, let's-make-fun-of- Marta event," she snapped. Noticing the plate of peach kugel on the kitchen table, her frown softened. "Thanks, Mom." She sat down, placing her notebook and pencil next to the plate and forked a generous piece of her favorite dessert into her mouth. "Ready for the family project questions?" Lili nodded, and Marta swallowed, clearing her throat. "What was school like for you? And did people make fun of you for being weird?"

Her mom chuckled. "Being smart must have been more fashionable in my school. I already mentioned I was a diligent student and loved science. Gymnasiums are competitive high schools. Not everyone is admitted. Students must work hard and keep their grades high. I never had a lot of friends, but a few of my acquaintances were in that school also. I was quite shy and didn't say much at school. We wore uniforms, so comparing clothing styles wasn't an option. There weren't many Jewish students in that particular school. Occasionally someone would call me "Hymie" or "Kike", but I just pretended not to care."

"That would have annoyed me!" Marta retorted.

"In the long run, those remarks were quite insignificant. I would have been happy to stay at that school. I loved my science teacher, and there was a cute boy."

Marta pounced on this immediately. "Dad?"

Lili chuckled. "No, Dad came later. This boy's name was Klaus. We worked on a science project and spent a bit of time together, but I never saw him again after my school year was interrupted." All of a sudden Lili's heart palpitated. She took a deep breath. "I need to start dinner now. Should we continue tomorrow?"

Lili abruptly arose from the table, avoiding her

daughter's quizzical eyes.

What's Hungary?

Marta sighed as she flipped through her notebook. She still didn't have many answers, just more questions. Her mom's evasiveness frustrated her. She figured soon it would be her turn for presenting in English class. As she envisioned all 24 pairs of eyes focused on her, the butterflies in her stomach fluttered.

Sure enough, the next morning, after several more students shared about their grandparents or parents in the United States military, Mrs. Harris caught Marta's eye, "I know not everyone's parents were soldiers or descendants of those on the Mayflower. Who else would like to speak?"

Marta gulped. She might as well deliver her contribution now and get it over with. She faced the class from the front of the room, fixing her eyes on the back bookshelf. "My mother grew up in Budapest. She attended a special school called a gymnasium and wanted to be a doctor." Marta paused as she noticed a few hands waving in the air.

Mrs. Harris acknowledged Tom. "Where is Budapest? He asked earnestly. "I never heard of it." Several heads nodded in agreement.

Pulling down the wall map, Mrs. Harris used the yardstick to point. "Budapest is the capital of Hungary, a landlocked country located in between Eastern and Western Europe."

Mary called out, "Are people hungry there?" A few students giggled, and Marta blushed, but Mrs. Harris continued, "Nope. The name is Latin and has nothing to do with lack of food. The Hungarian people have a long and complicated history, many centuries longer than the United States.

Marta proceeded with her brief presentation and was surprised to see that most of her classmates, including Mary, seemed interested and attentive. Thanking Marta, Mrs. Harris reminded them to continue interviewing their families and then transitioned to Beowulf.

When the bell rang, Marta strode to the door, tucking her head down as usual. Mrs. Harris intercepted her. "Thanks for speaking up today. The class showed a lot of interest in what you said. It went well, didn't it?" Marta nodded, not willing to confess how hard speaking up had been. "We are all looking forward to learning more about your family."

Mrs. Harris bent forward to make eye contact with her student. "And Marta – I, too, used to live in Budapest."

Remembering Hurts

Alone in the classroom, Vivien's hands started shaking like leaves in the wind as a dark shadow threatened to engulf her. Why did she say that? The years in

Budapest had all but faded into oblivion. Threads of recollections sometimes persisted, but not even one photograph or keepsake, never mind a relative, remained. Budapest might be a historic and attractive city, but her own few memories of it were anything but beautiful.

As the next class entered, she shoved her thoughts back into the recesses of her mind, willing them to stay submerged. Who would have thought Beowulf could be so soothing?

At home she mentioned the conversation with Marta to Paul. She didn't expect him to understand her previous life, but he always listened patiently. Sometimes she envied the simplicity of his past. Paul was raised on a farm in upstate New York right next door to his grandparents. Milking cows, feeding chickens, flying kites, and fishing in creeks were part of his daily life. Even the War had little effect. Paul enlisted and was stationed in Edinburgh six months before everything ended.

For Vivien, Budapest was only the beginning of a decade of atrocities. It still amazed her that she and Paul's lives had intersected considering the contrasting worlds they originated from.

That night even the pile of essays couldn't distract her. Instead forgotten images of her childhood in Budapest and what followed afterwards bombarded her mind with a cacophony of nightmares.

FIVE

Budapest 1943 - 1944

Vacation

Fritz slammed the shop door closed. It was Friday evening in June. Nine glorious days of freedom beckoned. Fritz liked stamps, but this job in *Vater's* shop was too mind-numbing for an active 18 year old. Their small, dark, and damp rented space felt like a dungeon. The regular customers, ancient men locked into the unglamorous realm of stamp collecting, produced lengthy discussions and infrequent sales. The ones with yellow stars on their coats appeared perpetually terrified. The others cast disdainful scowls as soon as they noticed Fritz's star.

Fritz had welcomed his family's recent move to Budapest, necessitated by his father's attempt to revive his stamp business. Budapest was much more cosmopolitan than Gyor. Its buildings portrayed a kaleidoscope of architectural styles including Neoclassical, Gothic, and Renaissance, the people a mix of Hungarians, Romani gypsies, Germans, and Slovaks. In some ways it was similar to Vienna since they shared so much history together. And like Vienna, the Nazi presence grew more conspicuous every day, and thus the lives of Jews living there grew more restricted.

The thing Fritz enjoyed most about his new home was the Boy Scout troop. Different than his troop in Vienna, it too was more provincial and even cliquish. Yet within the group he made some genuine friends, Jewish and Gentile, who enjoyed musical and outdoor activities, including his current favorite – rowing on the Danube.

Tomorrow started a splendid vacation with this new group of friends. One of the boys, Feri, had an aunt with a pension, a vacation house, at Lake Balaton. Besides his Scout camping trips, this was Fritz's first outing without his parents. The prospect of carefree sunny days with friends, amidst the gathering storms in Budapest, elated him.

The boys arrived at the Lake Balaton resort, bouncing with anticipation. "Wipe that grin off your face, Fritz," Feri commanded. But he had the same grin pasted on his own face. Not only were the accommodations attractive – a quaint cottage facing the lake, but Feri's aunt had encountered a group of young women whose chaperone requested companions for her charges.

The eager boys approached the boat dock where the girls and their chaperone awaited them. A blur of new faces and earnest conversation filled the next few hours. Fritz was glad his Hungarian had improved enough to be his usual witty and flirtatious self. Tall, dark-haired Kaja attracted him at once. Serious and quiet, she showed an interest in answering his probing questions. However, when they later moved from the boat to the lobby for dancing to popular tunes on the phonograph, two things became obvious: he could not dance very well, but Feri and Kaja could. And they continued to do so together all evening. Fritz observed, sulking from a chair in the corner, consumed with jealousy.

The next day on the lake shore, Fritz sat alone for a while, continuing to indulge in pouting and self-pity. But the day was too gorgeous, and there were plenty of other girls besides Kaja. He joined the group in the chilly water. As they were all splashing about and diving for coins, he literally bumped heads with one of the prettier ones. Lili.

Remembering the Lake

Back home, Lili awoke with a smile spreading from her face to her whole being. She still couldn't believe it! The memories of the past seven days shimmered like a magical dream.

Fleeing the chaos and paranoia of daily life in Budapest for an entire week had been amazing in itself. Lake Balaton was serene and gorgeous, reflecting the bright sunshine which filled each day. Lili delighted in the comradery with her group of peers and days of leisure, swimming, boating, and hiking. The accommodations were clean and quaint. But the highlight above all else was Fritz.

Lili had noticed him the first day they arrived. His brown, wavy hair accentuated his sensuous green eyes. He wasn't boisterous like the limited number of boys she knew but seemed intellectual and sensitive, almost sulky when Kaja lost interest in him the first night. He looked like a mournful puppy as Kaja danced away with Feri. Kaja was Lili's best friend, but too quiet and serious, even though she could dance well. Lili knew she had much more to offer Fritz. She just couldn't get his attention long enough to convince him.

The following day on the beach presented an opportunity that Lili couldn't have dreamed of orchestrating. They were all diving for coins in the clear lake water when someone cracked into her forehead. As she surfaced, head already throbbing, she saw Fritz also grimacing, "I am so sorry, Lili." He helped her to a lawn chair and went to the kitchen to fetch ice for the growing bump on Lili's forehead. He looked so concerned. And so handsome.

"I am seeing stars!" she joked. "I must be in love." Fritz's cheeks reddened, but he chuckled and scooched a chair closer to her.

"Well then, I better learn everything about you," he said locking eyes with her.

They talked almost non-stop the rest of the week about everything imaginable. Lili had never felt so comfortable with anyone before, so known and so understood. So seen. She was astonished at the witty responses and deep thoughts coming from her own lips. The bump mended. And she was head-over-heels in love.

Now that the week was over, the fears and uncertainties of life in Budapest settled back around her. But she allowed the sunshine and memories to occupy the larger place in her mind, anticipating the next rendezvous with Fritz.

Leaving Again

Seven-year-old Vivien chattered with exuberance about her school day as she walked home with her mother and Fredrick. She loved the new book they were reading in class, and she bragged about getting the highest score on her arithmetic test.

Fredrick lagged behind them, kicking every little

pebble in sight. He had already announced earlier in the week that he hated Kindergarten, except for recess, but today even recess was terrible because Lorinc had won all Frederick's marbles.

On reaching their apartment, she saw her father, Peter standing at the top step. What was going on? He never arrived home before they did. When Vivien glanced at his face, her heart sunk. A gigantic scowl covered his usual stern features, and his eyes seemed both icy and sad. Her exuberance and Fredrick's fretting disappeared in an instant. Something was wrong.

"You must each pack a satchel now," he announced. "We've been told Budapest will no longer be safe for German civilians as the Russians continue to rapidly advance. There is a special transport to Spain, and I have arranged spots for the three of you. Spain is officially a neutral country, willing to help in unobtrusive ways. Unfortunately I cannot leave with you at this time."

Her mind spinning, Vivien tried to push down the rising panic. What was happening? Who were the Russians? Where was Spain?

Karin spoke up firmly, "I will not leave you, Peter. I am not afraid." She stroked his cheek, but he pushed her hand aside.

"You must," he continued. "We can't send the children alone, and the situation will soon be extremely dangerous here for Nazis and their families.

Cooperative people in the Spanish countryside are willing to house German women and children. I'll help you start packing." He turned his head, but Vivien glimpsed tears in the corner of his eyes. Was her father struggling too?

The next few hours flew by as Vivien packed her small suitcase with some clothes her mother had laid out. "Bring what you can carry," her father had said. But what about her Grimm's fairytale book? Scruffy, her tattered bunny? Munshi, her cuddly gray horse? Only Scruffy fit. Vivien didn't want to cry and upset everyone more, but the tears kept building up and threatening to flood over. Any questions she asked were ignored or rebuffed, so she swallowed the words and the fears.

Fredrick chattered away, like they were preparing for a vacation in the mountains, his anguish over the lost marbles forgotten. Vivien wanted to shake him and shout, "This is something horrible!" Where would they live? What about school? What would happen to their father? She wasn't sure she wanted to know the answers.

The drive went on and on, out of the city and through many kilometers of rolling farmland. Sitting in the back seat of their car, Vivien tried focusing on the views out the window, to force her eyes to stay open for a while, but the events of the day kept rattling around in her brain. Sleep was a welcome diversion.

She awoke from a deep slumber when the car came to a halt several hours later. Faint twinkling lights from distant farmhouses were the only things visible in the vast darkness.

"Where are we?" Fredrick whined from the back seat.

No one answered.

Next to their parking space on a large patch of gravel, Vivien could spot a few silent huddles of people standing by their valises. Peter pulled theirs from the trunk. "Do you have the papers and money hidden away?" he asked her mother. Karin nodded, pointing to a pouch sewn on the inside of her dress. "It will be more dangerous for you if I am seen here," he said, gesturing at his uniform. He hugged Vivien so hard that she thought it would break her in two. And perhaps it did. She watched her father embrace Fredrick and then her mother. "I will see you soon," Peter whispered. "Remember that I love you." Karin's tears were now flowing freely as were Fredrick's and Vivien's.

Within a few minutes of his departure back to Budapest, a large paneled truck arrived. The clusters of waiting people transitioned into a semblance of a line, papers and baggage in hand. Slow as cold molasses, papers were checked and places found on the benches in the back of the truck.

Vivien clutched her valise and her mother's hand, trying to ignore the clamoring from within her body. As their turn to enter the truck was imminent, she couldn't wait. "Muter!" she wailed. "I have to go to the bathroom. I've been waiting for hours. I can't…"

Karin reacted to the panic on her daughter's face. "Over there – that clump of bushes. I will wait for you inside the truck door."

Vivien nodded and sprinted to the bushes, barely arriving before her body released its burden. Cleaning herself with some leaves, she heard the truck engine rev up and its back door slam. "Muter!" she yelled.

Vivien was sure she heard her mother screaming from the back of the truck, but it rattled noisily down the road and soon disappeared from sight. She could not believe that she was left there. Alone. In the dark. Somewhere unknown and unfamiliar. So she did what any seven-year-old girl would have done. She curled into a little ball on the side of the road and sobbed in deep anguish until sometime during the night when all the tears were spent.

As the hours of night passed by, the first clear thought pushing through Vivien's exhausted brain was that she must stay on this road. Her mother and the truck would come back looking for her at any moment. If she fell asleep, she might miss them.

Vivien trudged along the rutted road in the direction the truck had travelled. Throughout the night she did not hear any vehicles, or any noises other than the chirping crickets. As dawn edged its way on the horizon, she heard a sound. A truck! As it neared, Vivien saw it was not the large paneled one which was supposed to be their transport, but a small battered pickup. She stood in the road, waving both hands in the air until the truck lumbered to a stop.

"I need help," Vivien said in her best Hungarian. The old farmer shook his head, and she tried again in German. He smiled. They must not be in Hungary any longer. She explained how her mother and brother were travelling to somewhere in Spain, and she had been accidentally left behind. She didn't know which place in Spain. She didn't even know where Spain was, and apparently the farmer, Tamas, didn't either. He offered to take her to his home, but Vivien didn't want to leave the road. "They will come back," she kept insisting.

Tamas nodded and gave her his coat and a wrinkled apple. "I'll be back with some food. Maybe I can find someone who has a better vehicle to drive you further down the road."

After he left, Vivien ate the apple and burrowed into the coat, dozing by the quiet roadside until she heard the chugging of Tamas's truck returning. Out of the passenger side popped a woman who looked like a babushka in Vivien's fairy tales. Tamas's wife, Luci, was round and rosy, her gray hair covered by a black kerchief, a white apron around her rotund middle. Her arms overflowed with treasures – socks, a hat, mittens, a scarf, and food – all kinds of glorious-smelling food. Luci took Vivien onto her ample lap as she dressed and fed her, clucking and fussing till Vivien felt like a mothered chick.

Another vehicle was approaching, coming from the direction her family had gone. Tamas waved it down. A young man stepped out of a delivery truck. Tamas explained the situation, and asked if he had passed a big panel truck while driving. "I've been on this road for quite a while and have seen nothing like that," he answered. "It's a very long way to the Spanish border, at least 2000 kilometers." Seeing Vivien's perplexed reaction he added, "I'll put inquiries out among other truck drivers. I know lots of them."

Vivien let the ever-present tears fall again and allowed Tamas to place her in his truck.

Now the Nightmare

1944

Fritz checked the mirror one last time and slicked back a few errant waves. He straightened his striped tie and flicked off some specks from his dark suit jacket.

Ready for a night at the opera! Who would have thought Budapest would be the destination for world-class musicians? Cultural life here flourished in spite of the war in the rest of Europe. A variety of food remained available; even traditional delights and rare delicacies could still be found if you knew where to look. There were no air raids yet, and even with some deported Jewish musicians gone, classical concerts abounded. Alliances with the Germans brought some advantages.

Lili shared his passion for music and for adventure. They spent many evenings at concerts and delightful hours boating on the Danube. Wherever the location, they would talk about anything and everything with great intensity for many hours. Fritz had found his soulmate.

The opera, "Aida," was one of Fritz's favorites, so the long line for tickets didn't detract from his festive mood. Once inside the majestic concert hall, he and Lili lost themselves in the wonder and beauty of the artistic creation. Set in Ancient Egypt and composed by Giuseppe Verdi, the music and costumes were particularly entrancing tonight.

As they exited Ancient Egypt and the grand opera house to the city streets, the scene changed, revealing a shocking spectacle. Screeching fighter planes flooded the sky, swooping low enough to reveal the swastika under the wings. It had finally happened.

Lili slipped off her fancy shoes, running in the shadows of buildings with Fritz to his apartment. His parents were glued to the radio, eyes filled with apprehension. "The German army has marched into Hungary. The SS is occupying Budapest," his father stated, the stark words contrasting with the panic in his face.

The nightmare had arrived.

Changes followed immediately. On top of the earlier restrictions, more invasive ones were now placed upon the Jews. Food rations were cut. Jewish bank accounts became inaccessible. Businesses closed. Jews in many locations were moved to isolated ghetto quarters. Summons to labor camps accelerated.

Since Hungary had been in cahoots with the Nazi's, the American Air Force bombed railroad facilities and warehouses in addition to the frequent Axis attacks. The Russian army continued to push westward.

Despite the new dangers (or maybe because of them) Fritz spent more and more time with Lili. Knowing each day could be their last added romance to their relationship. And urgency.

On one of their few solitary walks along the Danube River, they leaned over a quaint, ancient bridge, watching the smooth water flow.

"I have something to ask you," Fritz's voice shook and his hands were sweaty

"Like, we should get married?" Lili teased.

Fritz stuck his hand in his trouser pocket, pulling out his great-grandmother's silver heirloom ring. "Well, yes, we should." He slipped the ring on Lili's finger. She threw herself into his arms almost knocking him over the railing.

"I take that for a 'yes'?" Fritz chuckled.

"Yes," Lili declared.

When the summons arrived two days later, calling him to a forced labor camp at Jolsva, Fritz was not surprised. Many of his friends had preceded him. He was strong and able to work hard. It was better than the concentration camps they had been hearing about where people were seized and never returned. He packed his knapsack with much warm clothing and hoped all his Boy Scout experiences would help make this situation bearable.

He hated saying goodbye to Lili. Roundups for Jewish women were becoming more common, and the rumor was that labor camps were no longer the only destination for them either. As much as they believed in the permanency of their love, the reality was they might never see each other again. To Fritz, that thought was far worse than the threat of death.

Another Identity

Another rainy day. Lili longed to give in to the cloud of melancholy colored by Fritz's departure and remain in bed. But there was no time for such indulgences. The Hungarian Nazis were also starting to gather up Jewish girls. Last night her parents promised to come up with a workable plan to keep her safe.

On cue her mother shouted from downstairs. Lili sighed and pulled on her robe. Both of her parents were seated at the dining room table, an unusual occurrence for a weekday morning. Their grim faces prompted Lili to realize she might not like the plan they presented.

When Lili sat down, her father pushed a small pile of papers toward her. The tender look on his face tore any of her remaining defenses down. "Today, you are no longer Lili Shuman, but an attractive, rich young lady named Hilda Hautz,", he said with a tight smile, attempting to make this seem like a frivolous game. "You will be a governess helping your new family with their two little children. You are no longer Jewish. You no longer know us. You will now be safe."

The serious words and abrupt new direction of her life hit Lili like a fist to her stomach. She could hardly breathe. Her father rose and engulfed her in a tight embrace and the dam broke. All three of them were hugging, crying, and talking. Of course it was her practical mother who broke the spell. "Go pack your bags. You are to leave today."

"*Anyi, Apu*—what about you?" Lili asked. "What about Gabor?" Lili was thankful her parents had the money and the connections to protect her—but what about her brother—and them?

"We are too old for the Nazis to bother with." Her father's joking voice clashed with his serious eyes. "But Gabor was called to labor camp yesterday. He will be going to the Jolsva camp where Fritz is."

"Is he still here?" Lili asked. She couldn't imagine leaving her whole family without proper goodbyes. And Gabor had always been the anchor of her life.

"He's upstairs packing," her father said.

Lili left the papers on the table and rushed upstairs to her brother's room. Gabor was shoving clothes into an already stuffed valise with serious determination. Lili threw herself into his arms, feeling like a lost little girl. "It will all be fine." Gabor patted her head with uncharacteristic gentleness. "Fritz and I will take great care of each other. And you will be such a fancy Hilda you won't want anything to do with us again!"

"Oh, sure," Lili retorted. "Tell me, Gabor, how can I do this? Do I just become another person and leave everything I love behind?"

"Exactly," answered Gabor, "but it is just for now. Wars don't last forever. Before you know it, life will be just as it used to be."

But they both knew. Nothing could possibly be the same again.

SIX

Elmsburg, New York 1963

Only Coffee

From his office, Fritz heard doors slam as the factory workers headed out for the evening. Fritz sighed. He had already missed his usual train, and the pile on his desk of unanswered mail was daunting. Some trivial thing he had heard on the news at lunchtime triggered unwelcomed dark thoughts, clouding his brain.

Dialing home, he waited for his wife's cheerful greeting. Lili always tried to please him, no matter how she felt. Today was no different. Their conversation fluttered between light, brief, and unsubstantial. She told him his dinner would be waiting. Fritz returned to his pile of paperwork, his empty stomach rumbling.

A brisk knock at the door startled him. His secretary stuck her head in, extending a savory-smelling bag and a cup of coffee. "Thought you could use some nourishment, boss," she said.

"Thanks, Amy. Come on in." Probably a mistake, he realized too late as he pulled out a toasted onion bagel lathered in cream cheese. Amy liked to talk. A lot. Fritz did appreciate how easily she made him laugh, but he should attend to the heap on his desk and get home to his family.

Perching on the extra chair, Amy's black tailored skirt hitched up past her knees. "Try this new drink," she said offering Fritz a red can labelled 'Tab.' "No calories." He shook his head and Amy continued, nibbling on her sandwich. "Even my new puppy enjoys watching 'Bonanza'. He just stares at the screen. But last weekend I got home late from the party at Marv's Bar, and he had chewed up the TV Guide. Do you think he was mad about missing the next episode?"

Fritz chuckled. Occasionally he did wonder how different a life of parties and bars could be now. Or even what a season of being a carefree teenager would have been like for him twenty years ago.

This was dangerous territory. He stood, tossed the empty bag and cup in the garbage can and reached for his coat. Not too many commuter trains to Westchester remained for tonight. The stack of papers would have to wait.

"Thanks again," he said, surprised by the measured look she offered him in return as she preceded him out the office. It stirred up distinct memories of the ladies' man he had once been, years ago as a teenager in another world. The look – and the memories were not unpleasant.

He missed the express train to Elmsburg, so by the time he arrived home, the children were in bed. Uncharacteristically, Lili greeted him with a stony expression and stated his dinner was in the oven. When he told her he had already eaten, her shoulders slumped, and she turned her back on him without a word. Fritz surprised himself. Instead of giving her an extra hug or asking what was wrong, he turned on the television – and kept seeing Amy's face. And other memories he succeeded in stuffing inside. He was a tin man, stiff with shame.

Is There Hope?

Lili dumped out Fritz's leftover dinner food and rinsed off the dishes. Sometimes she wondered what would happen if she acted on her feelings. Like smashing a plate and screaming at the top of her lungs. Fritz frustrated her. He could be so charming, but he could also be like a brick wall – silent and immovable. She imagined kicking this wall ferociously. And the resulting pain in her foot. None of his charm

was directed toward her these days. Maybe it was going somewhere else.

Her days were so lonely, and she worked so hard
to please her family. The spotless house. The delicious
meals. But no one seemed to care. Fritz, Marta, and
Larry were wrapped up in their own busy worlds. Her
world was empty. And all her attempts to change
things flopped.

The conversations about her past with Marta were
stirring up memories Lili didn't like to think about,
not just because of the profound sadness it caused, but
also because of the choices she sometimes wished she
had the opportunity to re-do. Leaving her family in
Europe after the war. Quitting college. Moving from
the Bronx. Why couldn't she let the past stay in the
past like Fritz did? Why couldn't she move forward?

Marta had seemed genuinely interested in tonight's dialogue. Lili was grateful for this new interaction with her daughter, even though it was painful.
As she relived the days of leaving school and the dras-
tic changes that had occurred in her life, she couldn't
help being struck by the contrast to present-day life in
suburbia. It was hard to imagine her sheltered daughter who couldn't handle mismatched clothes or a
classmate's teasing, walking through those chaotic,
dangerous times in Budapest.

At the end of their conversation that night, Marta
looked at her mother with appreciative eyes and a

whispered, "Wow, Mom." There was still a lot more to tell. Soon her narrative would intersect Fritz's story with a sliver of storybook romance. That romance seemed worlds away. Lili had no idea how to proceed. With Marta or with Fritz. Or with her own life.

Winner or Loser

The next morning Marta woke up feeling cheerful, surprising herself. Things were changing at school. Some of the kids in her English class spoke to her during the day. They asked her additional questions, showing genuine interest in her family story. Then there was band. Marta enjoyed playing the clarinet. Her new solo, "Country Gardens", soared with thrilling elegance in her practice sessions at home. Even her father complimented her. Yesterday, Mr. Stone, the band teacher, moved her up to the first clarinet section with all the upperclassmen. Billy, who was a decent tuba player, noticed and congratulated her afterwards. She was also intrigued by Mrs. Harris's remark about living in Budapest and resolved to ask her more.

Her good mood lasted all the way to the breakfast table where Larry announced he had eaten the last English muffin, leaving her with burnt toast and runny eggs. Marta snapped at her mother, turning away before gauging her response. She thought her father would correct her like he often did, but he seemed lost behind the morning newspaper.

By the time the school bus arrived, Marta had sunk into her usual mood of biggest loser alive. Did every 14-year-old girl feel this way? She wondered if there was anyone to ask.

In Math class, the substitute teacher couldn't calm down the chatty students. Instead of trying to teach them the new lesson, she allowed them to work together in small groups. Marta was surprised and pleased when Billy included her in a group with his football buddies. One of them, Charles, was even better at math than Marta, and the period passed quickly with all their cheerful banter. She did feel sorry for the substitute, who unable to control the noise, sat at her desk looking close to tears.

Next period, Mrs. Harris greeted the students as they entered her English classroom. On the board was written YOUR PROJECT. Mary griped, "What now?" but with a smile. Everyone was enjoying these sessions.

Mrs. Harris explained the newest addition. "You are all doing a wonderful job researching your family histories. It has been so interesting for all of us, but after today, you will start putting your family's feedback into a project of your choice which will incorporate information you are learning in History class. At the end of the semester, you will share this completed assignment with the class and maybe even the whole school at a special assembly. Let's brainstorm a list of different options."

The ideas started slowly but then took off like a freight train: a written report, play, oral report, cartoon, family tree, radio show, movie, diorama, show and tell – as the list of possibilities expanded, the excitement level grew.

The discussion took up much of the period. Mrs. Harris said there was only time for one daily report and asked for a volunteer. "How about more from Marta?" Cheryl blurted out. Marta blushed while the class nodded. They listened to her mother's experience of leaving school and dealing with the increasing hostilities with rapt attention until the bell rang. Feeling fortified by her classmates' approval, Marta lingered by her teacher's desk. "Can you tell me about your time in Budapest?" she asked.

"Sure," Vivien Harris responded, "Let's do that someday soon."

No specifics. Just a breezy someday. Marta sensed Mrs. Harris might not mean what she suggested. And if truth were known, Marta was tasting a similar discomfort of her own.

Let Somebody In

This time the black cloud followed Vivien throughout the entire school day. When she stepped into the safety of Paul's car, it threatened to break open and engulf her.

Paul didn't even ask what was wrong. Instead of taking the expressway home, he turned onto the scenic, winding road that overlooked the Hudson River. He parked in a deserted picnic area. When they exited the car, he pulled his wife into a secure embrace as sobs shook her body. He held her tightly until the tears were spent, and she relaxed. Wiping her eyes and grabbing his hand, they set off on the trail that snaked along the bluffs over the river.

"I want you to know, Paul," Vivien stated, "I am happy. I love you. I love teaching. I love our life together, but sometimes the horrid monster of my past rears its head. Today it overwhelmed me."

Paul chose his words with care, rubbing his wife's shoulder. "You lived through challenging, painful years, more difficult than I could ever imagine. It's only natural to mourn everything you have lost."

"Yes," Vivien agreed, "I miss my family terribly. But there's so much blackness and hurt in there – things too awful to put into words." She paused, gazing at her husband. They had such a close, honest marriage, yet this chapter of her life should be kept hidden away, even from him.

Paul squeezed her hand, "Maybe instead of telling me, you need to talk to someone else, a professional who can help you deal with the trauma of your past."

"You mean, like a shrink?" Vivien countered. "How could that help? The people who did these things aren't even alive anymore."

"All that hurt, pain, and bitterness are buried deep in your heart and mind," he answered. "And it's eating you up inside."

The conversation stopped as a deer scampered in front of them on the path. But Vivien knew Paul was right. It was time she unlocked that door, letting somebody in. If the truth came out could she finally be free?

That night long buried memories surfaced as Vivien struggled to find sleep. Her mother and brother. The truck. Her father. The mountains. The foster homes. None of them permanent but not awful. Narrowing into that One.

15 year old Vivien sipped the hot cocoa her foster mom had left on the night stand. Together with the down comforter wrapped around her, warmth started filling her whole body. After all these years, could this one in Lucerne, Switzerland be her forever home?

Unlike her other placements, she was the only child here, and both adults seemed attentive. Sometimes almost too much so. Setting the cup down, she turned off the lamp and snuggled into the soft bed. Minutes later, the door edged open quietly and then closed. She could smell her foster dad's cologne as he perched on the edge of her bed. He reached out a hand, patting her head gently. Then without a word, pulling off the covers he abruptly climbed on top of her, suffocating her with beer breath and his heavy body. His fleshy hand yanked up her nightgown and then smothered her screams, and she blacked out in the midst of the searing, unexplainable pain. And then the next night. And the next.

The only way to survive was to be silent. And completely numb. There was nowhere to go. No one to tell.

Today in History

Swallowing the last bite of lasagna, Marta picked up her tray and joined the swarm of students leaving the cafeteria for fifth period. "History?" Peggy asked.

Marta rolled her eyes. "Yes, and today we hear about our World War II projects."

"How about a toothpick model of a battleship?"

Marta snorted, "Right. Just be glad you are taking Civics."

On the blackboard in the history room various ideas were listed. People could sign up for their choices in pairs or small groups. Including battleship models. As Marta slid into her seat, wondering who she could sign up with, the teacher passed around mimeographed sheets and started explaining details of the projects.

She was interrupted by the intercom. "Attention." The class snickered as the usual static filled the room.

"Attention." The solemn tone of their principal's usual jovial voice stopped the chuckles.

"Forty minutes ago, our President Kennedy was shot in a motorcade in Dallas, Texas. He died in the hospital. Please pray for their family and for our nation."

Everyone froze. Marta's stomach somersaulted. Her teacher's horrified, pale face gawked at her students. "Class…" No one made a sound. No one moved. Tears covered everyone's face. Life had just stopped.

Marta knew this was a moment in history none of them would ever forget.

SEVEN

Budapest, Hungary 1944

Lili Again

"So much for being Hilda Hautz. I sure enjoyed the six months it lasted. Too bad the Hautz family got nervous about my false identity," thought Lili. She had delighted in her governess job in the wealthy Hautz household which allowed her to participate in the still bustling social life of the Budapest elite – dinners and parties with excellent food and plentiful drink. Entertaining Nazi officers felt risky but exhilarating in a strange way, especially when she had the opportunity to flirt and then rebuff their romantic advances. She knew she would never see them again. Nazi officers didn't patrol city streets.

As Lili filled the battered valise with her same old clothes, she decided to "borrow" the navy tailored coat Mrs. Hautz had purchased for her to use there. Tomorrow would be soon enough to again don the old shabby gray one with the conspicuous yellow Jewish star sewn in front. Or maybe the blue coat could be her permanent disguise.

Walking along the winding, almost deserted streets, Lili forced confident nonchalance onto her face. Much had changed in this section of Budapest, blocks away from the Hautz's upscale neighborhood. Nazi occupation was obvious. Swastikas adorned every building. Cars and trams were almost nonexistent. Few residents were shopping or walking about as Hungarians loved to do. Results of bombings abounded with rubble piled in front of damaged buildings. Many windows on the remaining stores were boarded up. The few civilian faces she saw seemed etched with fear.

Lili checked the slip of paper for the address her mother had given her on her last visit. She would be staying at a boarding house on the Buda side of the Danube River with her mother, *Anyu,* and other Jewish refugees. Her father was… Lili choked back a sob. According to her mother, her beloved father and many of their male relatives had been sent to a labor camp the previous week. One in Germany this time. There were so many rumors. Rumors Lili couldn't bear to contemplate.

Later that night Lili had settled into her small section of the new quarters when the air raid sirens screeched, piercing through any semblance of normalcy. Lili followed her mother and the other residents to the basement shelter where everyone huddled under blankets on the concrete floor. The Allied bombings must be frequent here as the rest of the residents ignored the chaos and before long were asleep. Except for Lili. And one very hungry infant who kept nursing and fussing throughout the night.

Soon she and Anyu settled into yet another cadence. Try to find food among the limited selections in the shops or on the black market. Try to fall asleep and ignore screeching from the skies. Try not to despair. Don't ask too many questions. Or think too much.

The brightest spots were her occasional rendezvous with Fritz. Lili replayed these scenes over and over again. The labor camp allowed him monthly leaves. On those days, right before sunset, she would venture out to the small apartment where his parents now lived. She still had her borrowed coat and false papers in case she was stopped. They would visit in a quiet corner or take a brief walk on a street where they could blend into the shadows.

The minutes flew by. Intense discussions about politics, literature, the future—anything—were punctuated by pauses for frequent kisses. Even though they didn't know what was around the corner, the danger of walking in Nazi-infested streets and repeated bombings didn't threaten Lili or Fritz. They shared the challenge of staying alive, the thrill of defeating the odds, even a sense of constant adventure. With each good bye, Lili reminded Fritz with a touch of drama of her memorized mantra, "I can't die; I have not yet really lived. A love as big as ours can't end in death without finding fulfillment and purpose."

Last month during one of their housebound visits, Lili's frustration had boiled up. "I can't stand the way your mother is always following us around and eavesdropping," she hissed to Fritz in a rare moment of privacy. "She gives me the evil eye every time I touch you."

Fritz snickered, "I am her only precious child. I suppose she might be jealous. Or worried that you will sweep me off my feet and whisk me away."

Lili didn't see the humor in his remarks. "Do you know Pig Latin? It can be our secret language."

After some practice, Lili and Fritz mastered giving and receiving endearments that only they could decipher.

And somehow, amidst all the deprivation, they each found books scattered here and there. For Lili, and Fritz too, books became a substitute for nourishment. After a book was devoured, they discussed it and traded it for another one. Fritz overcame his aversion for all things Hungarian and fell in love with its poetry. When he recited snippets of these to her, Lili's heart melted.

On this day, Fritz planned on visiting her at the boarding house. Lili put on her flowered peasant blouse and found a few ingredients for an imitation of *Kaiserschmarrn*, Fritz's favorite dessert of sweet pancakes. Maybe later they could sneak out alone for a walk along the Danube.

But as soon as Fritz stepped into the doorway, the sirens shrieked. Grabbing the pancakes and their latest book, Lili and Fritz scrambled downstairs to the basement, hoping they could enjoy both luxuries without sharing either of them with the residents of the shelter. Lili claimed her usual corner which was no longer private. The continuing superficial conversations and the hungry baby's shrieks seemed more suffocating than usual. Yet here they were—still alive, warm, and protected. And they were together.

Sharp knocks on the heavy wooden door broke through the chatter. Before anyone could respond, the door was shoved open revealing three Arrow Cross, the Hungarian Nazi soldiers, pistols raised. "We need a volunteer," the tallest one barked. No one looked up. No one responded. Utter silence. "If we don't have a volunteer, we will just shoot you all," the soldier said evenly.

Lili felt Fritz rustle beside her. And then—he stood up. Before she could grab him, he was striding out the doorway, following the soldiers. The door slammed shut. Lili was left behind. With dread like a fishhook in her heart.

Close Calls

To Fritz, his decision was either an act of utmost bravery or sheer stupidity. But the choice was being killed alone - or being killed with everyone else in the shelter. He remained silent as he followed the three soldiers through the dark streets accompanied by occasional sounds of artillery fire and tracer bullets. Arriving at their destination, Fritz's heart sank. This squat, gray building was the headquarters of the Arrow Cross, notorious throughout Budapest as the place where Nazis tortured abducted Jews.

The tallest soldier pointed to huge bags of flour stacked higher than his head. "Move these all to the storage room," he commanded and motioned another green-shirted soldier to guard Fritz. The unwieldly sacks were too heavy to lift, so Fritz dragged them clumsily across the uneven floor. Even this was strenuous.

After hours of hauling bags, Fritz dripped with sweat, and his muscles screamed in protest. The pile of bags didn't seem to diminish. As he mopped his face with his sleeve, he stumbled, falling to the ground and fainting. When he came to a few minutes later, the green-shirted soldier offered him a drink of water and then motioned for Fritz to follow him. They left the building, entering again the deserted streets towards the Danube. The Danube River where prisoners were often dumped and disposed of. Was this the end? But they continued to walk through the silence of the evening, away from the banks of the Danube.

In his numbed fear it took Fritz a few minutes to realize that they were again standing in front of Lili's apartment shelter. The soldier handed him a small, flat package and left without a word. Fritz tiptoed down the basement stairs, sure that everyone must be sleeping. When he entered the basement, Lili leapt up, her pale face as startled as if she was seeing an un-earthly vision. "I didn't think I'd ever see you again," she cried, meeting Fritz with open arms and enfolding him against her heart.

Fritz embraced her in return, nuzzling her hair with his chin. "I didn't think so either. It's been a very strange night." Late that night, after the all-clear signal allowed them to return to their apartments, Fritz was even more mystified when he opened up the wrapped package and found a slab of bacon—an unheard-of delicacy, welcomed by this non-Kosher family. Who was that man? And why had he risked his life to rescue Fritz? The questions transitioned to sheer gratitude. Fritz figured he'd never know but vowed to forever recall that memory every time he ate bacon.

It was hard to leave Lili and the relative safety of the basement shelter the next morning. As he said his goodbyes, Fritz's thoughts played the same repeating theme. How many close calls could he manage?

He boarded the train for the two and a half hour ride to Jolsva, clutching his precious pass and thankful again that he was working in Hungary. From everything he had heard, the Hungarian labor camps offered much better conditions than those in the Soviet Union or Germany. Its conscripts had a higher rate of survival even than those in military service (which was prohibited for Jews anyway).

Still the living conditions at his camp ranged from primitive to miserable. Fritz's Scout training provided a distinct advantage in attitude. Then they had chosen primitive camping as a fun activity! He could manage a solid night's sleep on the jute bags stuffed with straw, lined up on the floor of the large barn-like building where everyone was housed. Meals consisted of soupy stew and half a loaf of dark, dense bread, never tasty, worlds away from remembered Viennese cooking, but always filling.

A few days following his return, an unmistakable

whistle greeted Fritz after lunch. "Gabor!" he exclaimed, enveloping Lili's brother in a bear hug. "I've been watching for you, hoping you'd get placed in my detachment."

Fritz's muscles progressed from sore to strong as the two of them spent hours digging ditches two meters deep. Gabor's cheerful banter made the monotonous days of meaningless labor more bearable. "Are these potholes going to stop Russian tanks?" Fritz asked Gabor, tossing another shovelful of the hard-packed dirt.

Gabor gave a dry laugh. "These ditches are as useless as a glass hammer. Maybe we should toss in a handful of nails to puncture their tires. Or perhaps the soldiers will just die laughing at the sheer stupidity of our project."

Fritz could write daily postcards. The frequent mail arriving from Lili and his parents poured out discouraging news. The space allotted for Jews to live kept shrinking alongside with their rights. At the same time, more Hungarian ghettos were being emptied out and more inhabitants loaded into cattle cars. According to rumors, these were being shipped to concentration camps in German-occupied Poland.

Rumors also circulated at his camp. Some labor battalions like theirs, were being shipped to Germany, a frightening thought to each of them. Who would go where? What was the next destination? Their camp in

Jolsva was a gorgeous forested spot in the Carpathian Mountains. The guards – old and tired reservists – showed no desire to push or regulate them. Would the next place be worse?

When Fritz and some of his comrades loaded onto a cattle car in early May, the unknown of their destination clouded the sunny mountain morning. Gabor was nowhere in sight. But their car held 30 people instead of the 80 or more reported to be on most transport trains. Each day the train stopped several times in the countryside, so they could relieve themselves and get fed from a field kitchen. "This isn't as bad as I expected," Fritz kept reassuring himself.

After a long journey with many stops and engine changes, they arrived at Mizsepuszta, a small farming community that was thankfully in Hungary, still free from excessive Nazi harassment, instead of Germany or Poland.

After an initial introduction, the stern commander remained invisible when they were laboring. Fritz was assigned work that he never knew existed. Rather than digging ditches, their work was now farming, usually harvesting peas, moving across the field, rolling up vines like a carpet in front of them. Potatoes were uncovered by primitive machinery and then collected by the men with their sore, dusty hands. Fritz didn't mind this work. His misery was the straw bedding infested with multitudes of fleas. In the morning the men would step outside the barn shelter to the cold air and pick the numb fleas from their clothing before the day warmed up. Despite all the harvested food, meals were sometimes inadequate.

The commanding officer satisfied his love of military discipline by scheduling assemblies and calisthenics for the bone-weary men. And on one amazing day – August 20th – Saint Stephen's Day, the birthday celebration of Hungary's first king, the commander summoned the prominent musicians who had special privileges in this camp. They played the Intermezzo from "Calvalleria Rusticana" – a very moving, solemn piece and one of Fritz's favorites.

Despite these improvements, Fritz was frustrated and lonely. He missed the comradery of Gabor who had been sent somewhere unknown. Fritz missed his parents. But more than anything, he missed Lili.

Fritz learned his parents were forced to vacate their apartment in order to move in with another family across the street, leaving their furniture and most belongings behind. He couldn't imagine his mother coping with this lack of privacy and the loss of her special possessions. Their attempts to blend in with Gentiles didn't seem to be working as well as earlier, even with his mother's dyed blonde hair and strong German accent.

*****

As soon as Fritz adjusted to Mizsepuszta, rumors of relocation started once more. This time a freight train transported them to the Buda side of the Danube, to work at a nearby airport. Here an abandoned synagogue housed them. The living quarters were better but the work more difficult. Filling huge bomb craters left by Allied air forces using only shovels again seemed inefficient and futile. Whenever an air raid alarm sounded, Fritz and the other slave laborers had to lie down in the open field watching the overflights and dog fights. Hungary's military situation rapidly deteriorated as attacks by Russian, American, and British air forces intensified.

But as their muscles continued to harden, Fritz noticed the guards here were becoming much less vigilant, even friendly at times. Day passes were often available, and when they weren't, the men would just climb over the low boundary fence, undeterred, walking to Buda or Pest for a visit. Fritz decided to go and see his parents and Lili.

Emboldened by his first successful escape from the airport camp, he visited them often, always careful to return to camp by bed-count. Yet Fritz wondered continually how long his luck would hold out.

Wolfsberg, Austria

As eight-year-old Vivien stepped out of the chicken shed, the morning sunshine warmed her bare head. Each day of these six months on Tamas's farm were defined by the routines of milking cows, gathering eggs, and harvesting garden produce, along with the necessary household chores. She worked many hours and often wondered how Tamas and Luci had gotten along without her help. They lavished constant appreciation, affection, and attention on her.

The time Vivien was spending outside had reddened her cheeks. Her body had become sturdy and muscular. But inside, desperate sadness and worry reigned. Would she ever see her family again? Where were they? How would she find them?

Every few weeks the delivery truck driver, Moritz, stopped by offering news which was always the same. No one had seen the mysterious paneled truck which had transported her mother and brother away. No one could answer his questions about it.

Stumbling over some pebbles on the path, Vivien tripped, spilling her straw basketful of eggs. As she rearranged the undamaged eggs in the basket, she heard the familiar rumble of the delivery truck. Vivien sprinted to meet it, anticipation rising in her heart. When she arrived at the cottage, she saw Moritz on the porch talking to Tamas and Luci. Even though she couldn't hear the conversation, Vivien knew something was wrong. When she joined them on the porch, Luci drew her onto her lap, and Vivien covered her ears in anticipation of awful news.

"Small pieces of the paneled truck were discovered near the Spanish border," Tamas said, compassion filling his eyes. "There seemed to be a fire or perhaps a bombing. Bits of clothing were also found. It appeared no one survived."

Luci held Vivien tight, stroking her hair as sobs racked her small body. Vivien's imagined terrors had come true.

Hours later when all her tears were used up and silence filled the farmhouse under the evening sky, Vivien poked her head out from under the covers. In the stillness of the countryside, a distinctive bird call rang out, one she hadn't heard since leaving Berlin. Vivien remembered summer evenings in the park, her father expertly pointing out specific birds and their songs. She was certain this one was a nightingale. And it seemed to be sending her a message. Vivien had been so focused on waiting for her mother to return that she forgot her father could be alive in Budapest.

The next morning while munching on Luci's bread, *Schwarzbrot,* spread thick with apricot jam, Vivien told Tamas and Luci she wanted to look for her father in Budapest. They nodded solemnly, but when she reminded them that he was an important Nazi officer, both their expressions clouded over with uncertainty.

"My truck could never make it to Budapest," Tamas said. "Perhaps Moritz knows of someone who could take you. But Budapest is a very big city filled with many Nazi soldiers. How would you find your father?"

Vivien frowned. She tried to remember the name of her street but could only picture what it looked like. "I can draw a map," she suggested clasping her hands under her chin.

"Well, we have several weeks before Moritz shows up again. You can work on your map until then," Luci said, exchanging a concerned look with her husband as Vivien headed to her room. "How can we relinquish this precious child? I love her like my own." Luci choked back the sobs.

Tamas stroked her head, "But *Leibling,* she is not our own. And I forgot about the Nazi officer father. This could be interesting."

As Vivien labored over her map, her longing to see her father competed with her intense sorrow over the probable loss of her mother and brother. Thoughts whirled around her mind. "It is so peaceful here, and the chickens need me. So do Tamas and Luci. And they love me, lots. What if I can't find my father? Or what happens if he doesn't want me now?"

When Moritz checked in a few weeks later, the map was finished, and hope tiptoed around Vivien's mind. "I can't take the time to go to Budapest," Moritz said, sympathy etching his face. "But I do know someone who has that route. I'll see him tomorrow and ask if he could take you."

Sure enough, two days later, a black, battered van clattered over the bumpy road to the farmhouse. The driver, Latzi, introduced himself as Moritz's friend. "I'm heading to Budapest for a delivery," he said. "I have room for one passenger."

Vivien realized that once again, her life was going to change.

Do Something

Fritz was restless. Work at the labor camp was scarce. Bombings were frequent. It was obvious from watching the planes that the Russians and Americans were continuing to advance, and the Hungarians were panicking. He wanted to *do* something instead of waiting to be the next victim.

Each time Fritz left Lili or his parents, he felt it might be their final farewell. His father was in danger of being taken away to a labor camp once again. The

Hungarian government was under increasing pressure to "solve" the Jewish problem. The possibility of being sent to a concentration camp hung over all their heads. Everyone knew Jews were being killed there. And in other ways also. He and Lili each obtained a capsule of cyanide. They resolved to choose their own method of dying if captured.

Gulping down his meager camp breakfast of dry toast and weak tea, Fritz noticed Andras, one of his new companions, eyeing him. "I have some news,"Andras whispered when Fritz plunked down on the bench next to him. "The Swiss are now issuing additional *Schutzpasses*. We can collect them from their Vadasz office in Budapest and probably get enough for our whole detachment."

Fritz pondered this. For quite a while, his parents had been attempting to obtain *Schutzpasses* from Raoul Wallenberg, the Swedish representative who was committed to helping Hungarian Jews. These documents were a protective passport which offered a present safeguard from labor or concentration camps and eventual sanctuary in the issuing country. Switzerland, the Vatican, Spain, and Portugal granted similar concessions.

"What must we do?" Fritz asked. Here was the opportunity for action!

"Just get everyone's service identity papers. We'll put them in your briefcase and sneak out of camp in the morning."

At daybreak Fritz met Andras by the gap in the fence the workers used for their 'escapes.' As they entered town, they split up. Fritz slowed to a nonchalant stroll, thankful again for his Aryan features. Arriving at the Vadasz office, he safely joined the long line of Jews waiting for paperwork in front of the large, engraved wooden door.

All of a sudden, he noticed commotions at both ends of the narrow street. Military police had sealed off all exits. Fritz and the hundred or so people in line were herded into formation and marched with military escorts through the city. Fritz was panicking. He held the briefcase with the identity papers from his detachment What could he do?

As their little parade approached an intersection, Fritz saw his opportunity. A streetcar approached from behind them. Fritz motioned to Andras who had just joined him, and they stepped sideways out of the ranks. With the streetcar separating them from the marchers and hiding them from view, they clambered on to the still moving vehicle. Unnoticed. They returned to the camp shaken, briefcase intact with all the ID cards, but no passes.

By October 1944, Russia's Red Army had entered Hungary from Romania and occupied Debrecen, an important city on the Hungarian plains. The Allied

Forces were rumored to be offering a separate peace to the Hungarian government. Would this be the change they were all hoping for?

A few days later Fritz was ready for another outing, this time to visit his parents. He decided to risk spending the night with them, expecting that the next morning their status would change drastically, and they could celebrate their new freedom from the Nazis together.

As they gathered around the radio before breakfast, the news they had anticipated was instead, disastrous. German troops had retaken control of Hungary and imposed a state of emergency. All Jews were ordered to stay inside. Any labor workers not in camp would be considered deserters and shot on sight. The broadcaster warned that Arrow Cross militia were roaming the city, setting up road blocks, checking identity papers, and searching apartment buildings.

This presented a dilemma. Staying in the apartment jeopardized him and his parents. Traveling on the streets to return to camp was foolish. Fritz watched his mother's silent tears, his stomach churning. Why hadn't he stayed at camp?

As Fritz paced the small living room, the bedroom door opened, and out strode his father dressed in his World War I officer's garb. They locked eyes. Would this ancient uniform still be respected by any patrolling Nazis? Fritz, overwhelmed by his father's courage, kissed the top of his mother's head, and stood to follow his father. "Head up, shoulders back, we love you," his father whispered as Fritz matched his stride – from the apartment, unseen by any neighbors, through the silent war-torn streets filled with rubble, past the boarded up windows and shops, staring straight at the unknown fearful faces they encountered – all the way back to the camp without anyone questioning the outdated uniform.

Throughout the following tumultuous days, Fritz's division stayed put, waiting to see what would happen to them next. The news from postcards and radio broadcasts became increasingly disheartening. His mother wrote that his father was taken again to a labor camp and developed severe digestive problems. And then a few days later he heard many of the Jewish men left in Budapest were rounded up and marched to the Mauthausen concentration camp in Upper Austria. Stragglers were shot. Many died in-route of hunger or exhaustion. Lili's father and uncle Miklos were rumored to be among them. Fritz teetered between fear and frustration.

During this time, word came that against all odds, Wallenberg had pressured German officials to honor the *Schutzpasse,* using every legitimate and even unconventional means he could muster. Fritz's mother sent word she had received the family's passes and would get a Gentile friend to deliver one to Fritz and one to his father which gave them official permission to return to civilian life and protect them during the process. Overwhelmed with gratitude, Fritz prepared to make the journey to his parent's apartment.

A week later when several buildings were designated as safe houses by the neutral legations and the Hungarian Nazis, Fritz left the unguarded camp and with his parents moved into a small efficiency apartment prominently displaying the Swedish flag. No one had much confidence that this safety agreement would last for long.

Oh Christmas Tree

Bracing against the chilly December wind, Lili wrapped herself tightly in the navy coat. With her false papers in an inner pocket and her hat pulled low over her face, she figured she might as well be "Hilda" for as long as she could pull it off. She joined the festive-loving Hungarians who were determined to have some kind of Christmas celebration as they roamed the shopping areas in search of something to buy or trade despite the dangers that surrounded them. Avoiding the more crowded roads in favor of the meandering side streets, Lili kept the small, scraggly Christmas tree she had acquired, planted under her arm. Overhead bombers were screeching, even in broad daylight. Was she more frightened of being a target or of being recognized as a Jew? Neither, she decided. Fears should not ruin this special day.

Fritz and his parents would be delighted to see this Christmas tree, bedraggled as it was. Lili was thankful for the generous dab of goose liver her mother obtained on the black market which Lili used in trade at the outdoor tree lot.

Lili hummed *Stille Nacht*, an Austrian and Hungarian favorite, and the only Christmas song she knew. Throughout her childhood her family and many other Jewish families had chosen certain aspects of Christmas to enjoy without celebrating the religious significance of the holiday. Lili smiled, remembering how before the War, the Christmas tree would almost fill their parlor. As in other Hungarian homes, it would stay undecorated until Christmas Eve. While she and Gabor slept, their parents worked their magic. The next morning the tree stood in glorious splendor, adorned with white tapered candles and foil-wrapped chocolates.

These days, decorative candles and chocolate ornaments were nonexistent. This tiny tree would be a reminder of enchanting things past and the expectation of delightful things ahead.

On the nearly deserted street Lili heard approaching footsteps. As her breath shortened, she shook her head to dispel the fear. Anyone was free to walk these streets in the daylight, looking at the few stores open for holiday shoppers. There was even a decent meat market at the next corner. And still – the footsteps sounded menacing and were getting closer. Lili quickened her pace and tried to calm her rapid heartbeat. She would not turn around. Suddenly a man's arm thrust out right in front of her. It was not the sleeve of a soldier but a rather dingy, grubby sleeve. The arm reached for the tree and attempted to yank it from her.

Lili bristled. This was her tree! Her Christmas hope. She held the tree firmly against her coat and sprinted towards a busier street, mingling with the crowds, away from the would-be thief. Lili's body relaxed in relief, and she even chuckled, grateful for all those years of trying to catch up to a speedy big brother.

She arrived at the apartment where Fritz and his parents lived, somewhat tousled, but triumphant. As Fritz's mother clucked her pleasure and set the tree in a container on the kitchen counter, Lili noticed the simple array of appetizers including a scoop of goose liver.

Lost and Found

Tamas and Luci packed the back seat of the black van

with blankets, crusty rolls, vegetables from the garden, dried fruit, and several crocheted stuffed animals. Vivien was wedged amidst it all. After many rounds of tearful hugs and kisses with them, she waved desolately until their figures faded into the dusty horizon. Latzi, the driver, didn't have much to say. That was fine with Vivien. She see-sawed between sorrow at leaving the farm, the excitement of finding her father, and the fear that nothing would ever be right in her world again.

She dozed intermittently through many kilometers of rolling corn fields and tiny villages. There were few other vehicles on this road. The rickety van created ample amounts of noise, but whenever they stopped, Vivien could hear lots of fighter planes overhead.

"What is your father's name?" Latzi asked abruptly as the villages and farmland started giving way to larger towns.

"Peter Schwartz," Vivien answered. "I drew a map of my neighborhood."

Latzi grunted, "I am going to try something else first."

Vivien didn't know what that meant. She wondered why this man was helping her. He wasn't at all pleasant. Why would he care about what was happening to her?

She noticed that buildings of all sizes and shapes

were packed close to one another, and more cars were travelling on the narrow roads. This must be Budapest, Vivien thought. She didn't recognize her surroundings, but then she had never ventured beyond her own neighborhood. In a few blocks the van stopped before a squat, gray building. Vivien recognized the Nazi flag and the Arrow Cross sign displayed in front. A soldier approached their vehicle. "No parking here," he barked with disdain, eyeing the battered van.

"We are here to see Peter Schwartz, Captain Peter Schwartz. This is his daughter, Vivien," Latzi said.

The soldier straightened up and snapped a salute. "I will see if he is available. You may wait here."

Minutes later Vivien saw a familiar figure, standing at attention in the doorway. "Papa," she called, as she opened the van door and jumped out.

The questions racing through his mind were swallowed up by overwhelming joy. Peter leapt down the stairs, engulfing his daughter in his arms as their bliss mingled together.

EIGHT

Elmsburg, New York 1963

Colleagues

The student monitor handed a slip of paper to Vivien.

"Can you please stop by my classroom tomorrow after school, so we can discuss our World War Two projects?" Anne Nelson.

Vivien scribbled, "Sure" on the paper even though she wasn't so sure about this meeting. As head of the History department, Mrs. Nelson appeared aloof, even imposing. They had yet to have a personal conversation, just notes about the family history assignments the students were working on in English and History class. Getting picked up later would also inconvenience Paul. However, as colleagues, they needed to cooperate and coordinate these projects.

But after school the next day, Mrs. Nelson greeted

Vivien with a warm, open smile and a plate of cookies. "Every adult needs a treat after a day with these hooligans. Have a seat." She gestured toward the padded chair by her desk. "And please excuse the mess. After all these years, I still can't keep up with all the correcting."

Mrs. Nelson's wrinkled blouse, and her disheveled hair somehow put Vivien at ease. No perfection here either.

"How is it going with your students' research on their families? Oh, and please call me Annie. We are partnering together though this challenge. Discussing World War Two can bring up a lot of interesting reactions."

Vivien's breath hitched. Was this woman a mind reader? She decided to take the initiative. "Yes, I am seeing a lot of unique responses. How was your family involved?"

"My husband was stationed in Versailles, France as an ammunition specialist. Two years after returning home uninjured, he was killed by a drunk driver who was our neighbor," Annie said evenly.

Vivien's jaw dropped. "How awful. I am so sorry." She wanted to ask how one gets over something like that, but she didn't feel at liberty to ask such a personal question, even after such a delicate revelation.

Again, Annie must have read her thoughts. "It

was a very difficult time in my life. I struggled to forgive my neighbor, Fred, for many years." Annie glanced at the clock. "My goodness, here I am just chattering away about myself. We better use these last few minutes to go over our project collaboration. Can you meet again in a few days? I have some ideas for an all-school presentation."

Vivien nodded, her mind captured by that one word.

Forgive.

What Happened to Us?

Lili lifted the lid. The distinctive smell of Paprika Chicken wafted through the kitchen. One of the few recipes she had obtained from her mother, it required hours of chopping, sautéing and simmering the stewed onions, green peppers, tender chicken, sour cream, and plenty of Hungarian paprika. It was the family's favorite, and just what everyone needed on this chilly Thursday.

Larry arrived home first today, shouting an enthusiastic, "Yum!" as he headed to the snack drawer. "I don't have any homework. Can I go play baseball with the guys?" he asked, grabbing a cookie and vanishing when Lili nodded her assent.

He almost collided with Marta as she trudged up the stairs, arms loaded with books, forehead wrinkled, looking as usual like she carried the weight of the world. She did manage a smile and a muttered, "Smells good, Mom," before heading to her room.

"Marta," Lili called, "Why don't we spend some time on your project? Dinner is ready, and we have the house to ourselves for a bit." If they didn't talk now, Lili thought she might lose her resolve to move through her memories. She was almost looking forward to this part of the story, hoping that highlighting the normal, positive things from her past might keep the inquiries under control and satisfy Marta's curiosity.

Marta came into the kitchen, sat down, pulling out her notebook and pen from her knapsack. "Sure, Mom, I need a change from these last few days of focusing on President Kennedy's assassination."

"Let's see. I think I remember where we stopped. Life became more restrictive," Lili began. "I had to stop going to school. Other places like certain stores and offices didn't allow Jews. But Budapest wasn't as bad as most other places in Europe because Hungary had made some alliances with Germany. We could still attend concerts and take vacations at certain locations." As she proceeded to talk about the time at Lake Balaton and the developing relationship between her and Fritz, she noticed Marta's expression. She wasn't entranced by the account of this budding romance as Lili had expected but almost seemed skeptical.

Finally in typical Marta fashion, the words spilled out, "That just doesn't sound like you or Dad. What happened?"

"Well, be patient, I am getting to more of the story now," Lili said.

"No, I mean what happened to you and Dad?" Marta blurted. "If you were so much in love, how come it seems like now you don't even like each other?"

Lili's mouth hung open. Sure, she and Fritz had their problems. Didn't everybody? They attempted to not fight in front of the children and never to use English in their arguments. What was her daughter seeing?

Then, just like a cheesy movie, the phone rang. Fritz's voice was loud enough for both of them to hear – the words and the detached tone, "I won't be home for dinner. An urgent meeting just came up."

Lili couldn't meet Marta's eyes. She was grateful that Marta mumbled something about working on these notes and retreated to her room.

Lili sat at the table long after she removed the remnants of dinner and tidied the kitchen, thoughts swirling. What was going on with Fritz? Did she even want to know? Shrinking into her chair, she felt like only a shadow of that vibrant person she had been talking about. In reflection, that passionate, adventurous creature she was portraying to Marta didn't sound like the Lilli of today. Where was the person she wanted Marta to know and more important, to imitate?

Lili headed to the magazine rack in the living room. In between old New York Times magazines she found the Hunter College catalog she had stuck there weeks ago. Maybe this could be her ticket for moving forward. Something had to change.

What is Wrong?

With focused determination, Marta plowed through her piles of homework. Dinner had been pleasant enough even with her father's absence. She and Larry kept up a steady stream of cheerful chatter as they devoured the chicken. Her mother displayed her usual jovial smile. Yet Marta couldn't get the earlier image of her mother's pained face out of her mind. What kind of hornet's nest had she stirred up with her earlier outburst? Was something wrong with her parents' marriage? She wished for the millionth time there was a wise person to whom she could unburden her heart. Was there anywhere she could get some comfort? And answers?

Marta shifted the finished homework to her school bag, washed her face, brushed her teeth, and put on her flannel nightgown. It was late. Her brain felt trampled.

As she climbed into bed, she heard the front door open. Her father. Within minutes she heard her parents exchanging sharp words, English transitioning into Hungarian, an ominous crescendo.

Marta put her pillow over her head. She wished she knew how to pray. Instead, she cried.

Make it Work

"What did people do without newspapers?" Fritz mused as the inbound train zipped through Westchester County. Newspapers were both a distraction for him and a shield from all the nameless faces around him. The distraction part wasn't working well this morning even with the headlines declaring the highlights of the Warren Commission's first meeting investigating Kennedy's assassination. Lili's angry reaction last night had surprised him. Most of the time she tiptoed around his moods and excuses. In some ways her resentment made it easier, allowing him to feel justified instead of guilty. And she didn't even know the whole story. Shame was now the ground on which he walked.

He had not intended to have this involvement with Amy, fighting hard against it – at first. But life at home had become so dull and predictable. Lili never had anything interesting to offer in conversations, and they had no activities to pursue together. She managed the household and the children's schedules. And that seemed to be her entire world. Maybe enjoying this little "indiscretion" would help him to endure his marriage. Amy's flirtatious attention was exhilarating. It made him feel adored and charming again.

An ad in the corner of the third page caught his attention. A jewelry sale at Dixon's. Yes. A new necklace with a sweet card should calm the waters at home. He wasn't ready to wreck his marriage and upend his family. But he also wasn't willing to turn his back on this affair. For generations in his family, and even throughout history, he knew many men had maintained parallel lives with wives and mistresses. He could handle it too.

Finally Angry

Lili placed the receiver down, frowning at the phone. Registration at Hunter College had closed last week. She'd missed another opportunity to alter her circumstances. Again. Why had she waited so long? She knew the answer. She wanted desperately to believe that Fritz had changed this time. Lili fingered her new necklace, thinking about the pleasant conversations between her and Fritz these past few weeks. They had even taken some family outings to the zoo and the beach, rare but satisfying experiences.

But this last week, Fritz's sharp words had been sharper and his silences longer and more hurtful. Last night, Lili refused to overlook his behavior any longer. When she asked him what was wrong, he exploded. "I can't try anymore!" and stomped out the front door.

Of course, she lay awake, trying to figure out how she could fix everything. Many hours later Lili heard him come in and noisily settle into the guestroom across the hall. Towards morning, she fell asleep. Fritz was already gone when she went downstairs.

But her sorrow and hurt more often were turning into anger. Maybe that was good because she felt mobilized to do something. Anything that would make a difference. Something to get her unstuck.

Full-time classes for four years in New York City pursuing an education degree wasn't practical. Too much time commuting and being away from the children. So becoming a teacher seemed out of her reach. As she cleaned the kitchen and rehashed her options, Lili decided she would go to the library tomorrow and research other careers. Another dream to lay aside. Her anger and hope gave way again to a huge fog of insecurity, sorrow, and loneliness.

During dinner Fritz wouldn't meet her eyes. The children deliberately filled in the awkward spaces with superficial chatter about school. Once they left the table, Fritz scowled and in Hungarian said, "We need to talk."

Lili knew something unpleasant was coming. And she didn't want to hear it.

Normal Process

Fritz perched on the wooden stool in their bedroom, eyes fixed on the framed Rembrandt print on the opposite wall. "I can't go through the motions anymore," he stated in a flat, emotionless tone. "I need some time and space apart from you to figure things out." Fritz couldn't believe the clichéd words that were coming out of his mouth. But he also couldn't believe how little feeling he had left for this woman who had been his life partner for 20 years – years filled with hardships and victories, loss and success, adventures and family. What was wrong with him? Was it his youth as a "golden boy"? Was it what happened on their escape journey emerging from the shadows?

Lili sat hunched over on the edge of their bed, staring at her feet, and picking at the lint on her blue wool sweater. She didn't cry. She didn't beg him to reconsider. But she looked like she had been stabbed in the back by her best friend. And that's what he had done.

"Where are you going? What do we tell the children?" she mumbled.

"I rented an apartment in Hartsdale. We'll tell the children we are separating for a while, and that I'll be taking them out to dinner every Thursday. We might as well do it now." Fritz stepped into the hall and called the children from their rooms. He noticed their exchange of uncomfortable glances as they joined their mother on the bed. Lili's eyes were still fixed on the floor. It appeared he had to initiate this unsavory conversation alone.

"First of all, you need to know we both love you very much," Fritz said.

"That's why we can't work on our homework?" Marta interjected, rolling her eyes.

Setting his jaw and taking a deep breath, Fritz plunged in, sharing his plan to move out of the house for a while. The shocked looks on both children's faces were worse than Lili's reaction had been and almost softened his determination. But not quite.

When he asked if they had any questions, Marta gave the expected, "Why?"

Fritz bit his lip. "This is a normal process. Sometimes grownups need to be away from each other to work on their relationship.

Marta responded with sharpness, "Is that more important than being together as a family? "

He had no answer. The freckles stood out like drops of blood on Larry's pale face. Marta's was a thundercloud ready to burst.

After a few minutes of painful silence, Fritz kissed the top of their heads and motioned them to go back to their homework. Lili left the room also.

He pulled down the big red suitcase from their closet and numbly started placing folded clothes inside. If he didn't leave tonight, he would lose the remaining shreds of his resolve.

My Heart Hurts

Marta could not believe it. She didn't know anyone's parents who did this. What was going on? Would they actually get divorced? Not only was she too upset to study for tomorrow's Science test, but all her excitement about the band's first halftime show on Saturday had vanished. This was so unfair. School was finally enjoyable. Didn't her dad care about anyone else besides himself?

More tense-sounding words drifted up from downstairs. Turning up the volume on her radio, Marta tried to concentrate on physics theories, accompanied by the Beatles singing "I want to Hold Your Hand." She didn't hear her mom coming up the stairs or the soft knock, so the opening door startled her. Marta turned off the radio and looked at her mom. She expected to see tears, or anger, or – something. She didn't. Marta couldn't remember ever seeing her mom's face look so much like a blank slate.

"Do you want to talk?" her mom questioned. Marta didn't know where to begin. Any word could set off more disaster.

"Not now." Marta glanced at her mother, noticing her trembling chin and the tears starting to drip. She looked away. Neither one of them knew how to handle all this uncertainty and pain.

"I do love you," her mom said. "And remember, none of this is your fault."

"Great," Marta thought. "Then whose fault is it?" As soon as the door closed, her own tears came fast and furious. Answers and sleep would be elusive.

At the end of English class the next day, Marta approached Mrs. Harris. "Is there a time next week we could talk?" she asked. "And not about Budapest," Marta added.

I Found a Friend

Vivien strode with purpose into Annie's classroom, carrying a plate of *Pfieffernüsse*, the special German spice cookies Paul had helped her bake last night, and a typed list of all the projects her students had signed up for.

Annie greeted her at the doorway, grinning. "These look delicious. My grandmother used to make them at Christmas time. Are you German?"

Panic threatened to overcome Vivien's planned professionalism. She took a measured breath, setting the treats on Annie's cluttered desk. "Yes, I was born in Berlin. We moved to Budapest, Hungary, when I was five."

Silence sat. Comfortably.

Annie nibbled on a cookie, but her eyes radiated affirmation. And the door tumbled open.

"My father was a Nazi officer. He attempted to send my mother, brother, and me to escape to Spain before the Russians came to occupy Hungary. I got separated from my mother and brother. Their vehicle was later found destroyed. I never saw them again." Vivien bit her bottom lip, amazed those memories and emotions could still engulf her so completely. "There is a lot more to the story, but I can't..." She squeezed back a shattering sob.

Annie grasped Vivien's hands and looked straight into her eyes. "My dear girl. You too, jumped into a difficult topic. I think we need to schedule a whole evening for just the two of us. Wine and conversation. I'm a great listener."

Gratitude filled Vivien's heart. A kindred spirit. For her.

NINE

Budapest, Hungary 1945

Thank You, Mr. Wallenberg

The pungent odor of roasted chicory which had become the Hungarian *ersatz* coffee assailed Fritz's nose as he folded up his bedding in the corner of the living room and joined his parents in the kitchen.

Kissing the tops of their head, Fritz was struck again with how much they both had aged these last few months, especially his father. The worry wrinkles kept spreading on his face, the twinkle had disappeared from his green eyes, and his thinning gray hair revealed new bald spots. Just as Fritz added half of one of the last precious sugar cube to his hot drink, an impatient knock on the front door interrupted the morning chatter. Their eyes shifted to each other in panic. Dismay locked them into silence. Brisk knocks hinted at something terrifying.

Fritz opened the door to two Hungarian Nazis

soldiers in full regalia who without invitation stepped into the main room. "You and your father have ten minutes to pack whatever you wish to take with you," commanded the mustached one, eying each of them with a cold, piercing stare. Fritz's father's face blanched white. His mother clutched her hands on her lap, trying to disguise their trembling.

Fritz kept his eyes leveled on the soldiers. "I'll do the packing," he said in a calm voice, willing his parents to remain quiet and his own legs to move. He grabbed several layers of clothes for both of them and returned a few minutes later with a large blanket bundle. As he hugged his mother, he whispered in her ear. "We'll be back soon." She didn't look convinced. Fritz wasn't either.

In front of their apartment, Fritz and his father joined a group of men of various ages, most with similar bundles and fear-etched faces. Trudging through familiar neighborhoods, it became apparent they were heading to the rail terminal which nowadays had only one purpose –deportation to concentration camps.

Fritz's mind was spinning. He smelled sweat drenching his clothing as they passed familiar buildings, stucco walls in pastel colors – walls observing for centuries, impassive and silent. More men kept joining them until their marching unit filled the street, squeezing out the few frightened pedestrians. He had to try something. Soon there would be no options left.

"I'm going to drop our bundle and look for a way for us to slip out of formation," he mumbled to his father.

But the Nazis who were escorting them were numerous and vigilant. Before an opportunity came, the train station was in view. Fritz was panicking. If he was alone, he would have risked all to run for freedom. His father couldn't handle that kind of exertion, but he also couldn't endure a grueling train ride. And he would not survive concentration camp. All the weeks and months of plotting to avoid disaster seemed to be closing in on him, tighter than a noose around his neck. Fritz kept his expression blank as his thoughts continued whirling.

Arriving at the terminal, he observed the numerous, assembled cattle cars, large, metal sliding doors wide open, waiting to swallow up the crowd of detainees. With their guns, soldiers were motioning men aboard as dogs circled the reluctant passengers, snarling and nipping at their ankles. The cars were filling up. Still the size of the group didn't seem to diminish. More men kept marching in. Fritz pressed close to his father, swallowing the bitter taste of fear and defeat.

Suddenly a sleek, black car, exhibiting a Swedish diplomatic license plate and flying a small Swedish flag on the antennae, drove up beside the platform. A slim, blond young man emerged and hurried to the supervising officers, confidence oozing from his determined stride. As he presented documents to them, an animated discussion ensued with plenty of hand gestures visible to all those assembled. The loading process halted. After what seemed like hours to Fritz, the young man approached the railway cars to talk to those inside. In amazement Fritz watched people exit these cars to stand on the platform alongside his group.

"If you have a Swedish *Schutzpasse*, please present it now," the young man addressed them all in halting Hungarian through a bullhorn. "I am Raoul Wallenberg. I have the authority as a Swedish diplomat to take those of you holding these passes away with me and return you to your homes."

Clutching their precious passes, Fritz and his father flashed each other a stunned but grateful look and once more stepped out of what would have been certain calamity.

Over the Bridge

Each day, Lili found it harder to be optimistic. There was no word at all from her father. It had been months. Did this mean he was languishing at a concentration camp? Or was he already dead? Their apartment was tiny and claustrophobic. The strained relationship with her mother threatened to further unravel as they spent most of each day cooped up inside together with nothing much to do. Food was getting difficult to find. Last week it was only flour and dry beans which didn't lend itself to an appetizing menu. Lili knew Fritz was at the safe house with his parents. Across the Danube River, another world away.

Yesterday, from overhearing conversations on the street while she scurried on her food search, Lili surmised that the Russian Red Army continued to advance. Artillery shells and bombings were increasing. No one seemed to know how this development would affect the Jews, the Nazis, or the rest of the Hungarians, but everyone seemed more skittish than usual. The Russians had a worse reputation than the Nazis. Lili didn't understand everything she heard. She wasn't sure she wanted to.

As Lili heated up water for the *ersatz* morning coffee, the power flickered several times and then went out. Minutes later, air-sirens screeched, and the rumble of the bombers came closer, intensifying to a roar. The four windows in their apartment rattled, and then all of them shattered at once. Lili sighed, annoyance competing with fear and gathered up some necessities for their relocation to the basement shelter. Again. She shoved the blankets, pillows, and some clothes into a sack, handing a spoon and a bowl of lentil stew to her mother.

Following other disgruntled residents down the grimy stairs, Lili felt the building shudder. Cracks appeared and widened on the walls around them as chunks of plaster fell in the stairwell by their feet. This time the bombs had found their mark, close enough to raze their building. Lili's mother screamed—anguished, unintelligible sounds, face pallid, breath rasping, dropping the bowl with a clatter.

"*Anyu.*" Lili grabbed her mother's shoulder. "Come with me. This way now. Instead of going to the bomb shelter, we need to leave before the building collapses."

Her mother nodded, eyes glazed by fear.

Lili took her by the hand as they hurried out the front door. Who was the adult in charge? Her mother seemed to be crumbling inward just like the bombed apartments.

People were running haphazardly in every direction. The shrieks of children blended with the frenzied exclamations of adults. All focused eyes on the skies, unsure of where refuge existed from the monsters in the air.

Lili bolted toward the Margaret Bridge, only a few blocks away, dragging her mother behind her. Once they crossed the Danube, they'd be on the Pest side of the river, close to Fritz's safe house as well as *Anyu's* sister, Berzi's, apartment.

However, once they got partway on the bridge, Lili realized they had become exposed targets for the planes flying close overhead. People dropped like flies around them as the strafing gunfire found its mark.

They ran, *Anyu's* wrinkled fingers clinging to Lili's hand like rigid bands of steel, each desperate not to stumble over the unmoving matchstick bodies strewn everywhere.

In Lili's agitated mind, *How wide is this river* alternated with *Help, dear God.* The normalcy of the usual scenic stroll had become a living hell. Acrid smells of burning buildings joined the stink of her own sweat-fear, punctuated by the shrieks of the wounded and the deafening silence of the dead.

Somehow, they made it across the bridge. The sounds of the bombing and gunfire shifted to another direction. Lili hurried her mother through the four blocks to Aunt Berzi's house focusing on the cluttered ground and ignoring the ominous sky still full of planes while trying to keep them both as inconspicuous as possible in the panicked crowds. Even without their star bedecked coats, safety was never assured.

Lili could still feel her mother's whole body trembling as she supported her arm, whimpered moans escaping her clenched jaw. Nothing in *Anyu's* sheltered life had prepared her for being immersed in such disaster.

When they reached her aunt's apartment, Lili hugged her mother good-bye in the doorway. Her aunt could take charge of her mother. Lili knew they were both ready to collapse, but she couldn't deal with any more emotional drama and her mother's suffocating neediness. Her top priority now was to get to Fritz, to see for herself that he was alive and unharmed. She kept the farewell brief and unemotional. "I will see you soon," Lili said. With a final wave, she set off through three blocks of horror—demolished buildings, cobblestone streets covered with the dead and dying.

Once she made it past the unofficial guard at the entrance of the Swedish safe house and fell into Fritz's arms, all her fear and exhaustion dissipated. "You are here," Fritz kept repeating, squeezing her tighter and tighter. Nothing else mattered.

The following day on Fritz's parents' advice, Lili travelled on narrow, now quiet, side streets to the Swedish embassy for papers which would allow her to stay in this house as an adopted daughter. A new, unknown chapter.

Toys for Me

Vivien bounced on her chair, staring at the food for lunch Papa had left on the table, and then tiptoed in circles around the small apartment, running her finger along the plastered wall, counting the cracks. She was tired of being as quiet as a mouse like her father instructed every morning. Plunking back on the chair, she pushed the food aside and picked up the pencil stub, practicing a few more letters on the one remaining piece of paper. Next, she turned her attention to her tattered bunny, Scruffy, and the small baby doll her father had found. Picking them both up, she tiptoed to her secret place.

Behind the long, dark drapes in the living room, she could watch people bustling about in the city streets. Busy with each other and doing important things. But her days were slow and long. There was no clock. Nothing to do. No one to talk to. When Papa appeared each evening with food for their dinner, she would melt with relief in his strong arms.

The same story orbited around her mind. Over and over again Vivien told him everything that happened after he had dropped her mother, brother, and her off for the transport to Spain. Repeatedly he promised her that he was using all his influence to locate her mother and brother. He assured her that they might have survived. And when she slept curled next to him on the couch every evening, she could believe their situation would work out. Happily ever after.

Vivien's stomach grumbled, signaling lunch time. She nibbled on a hard roll, trying to make it last. After ten tiny bites, she allowed herself a tidbit of cheese. At the sound of a gentle knock on the front door, she froze midway through swallowing. Papa reminded her each morning not to open the door. No matter what. The knocking persisted, accompanied by some whispered Hungarian words. What should she do?

It was a woman's voice, a gentle, kind voice. Vivien sidled up to the door. "I am not allowed to go out or let someone in," she whispered.

"That's fine," the woman answered. "I just have some toys I want to give you. My little girl…" the voice choked up, "isn't here anymore. I see you at the window. But I have not told anyone about you."

Vivien opened the door a few centimeters. She could see a thin, black-haired woman with sad, brown eyes holding out a small sack which she slid through the crack. "*Köszönöm,*" Vivien thanked her. The woman nodded and disappeared around the corner.

After shutting and locking the door, Vivien took the sack to the table. With excitement she pulled out each marvelous treasure, one by one. First was a doll, not a baby doll, but a fashionable doll complete with a shiny silver dress, blue hat, fur lined cape, and high heels. Folded in a handkerchief were extra doll clothes – fancier, sparkling clothes and other accessories. Golden curls topped a lip-sticked smile. Vivien decided she must be a movie star and christened her "Marilyn."

Next, she pulled out books, beautiful picture books, but most amazing of all, the few words on each page were Hungarian words she could read. Last was a hoop with material stretched over it, a needle, and packets of different colored threads. Vivien wasn't sure what to do with that. She focused on Marilyn, dressing and undressing her and using containers from the kitchen to create a many-roomed house for her, humming bits of remembered German songs.

Vivien was so engrossed in her new toys, she didn't hear the front door open. "What's all this?" her father stern voice demanded.

Her body started trembling from her toes and moved up her body, shaking her inside and out. Vivien couldn't remember ever hearing her father so upset. "I didn't let anyone in," she tried to explain. "I just opened the door a tiny bit, and a lady passed me this sack of toys." Even to Vivien's young ears, this didn't seem like a plausible story.

Peter sighed, sitting down at the table, the anger in his face turning to worry. "I knew someone would notice you. I was just hoping we had more time." He stared at the ceiling, rubbing his forehead, considering his worries from every angle.

Finally, Peter pulled his daughter close and stroked her head. "Vivien, we will leave in the morning."

Surviving

The bombing was constant. Machine-gun fire and the thumping of mortar shells echoed in the deserted streets. The danger didn't rattle Fritz as much as the noise. The unrelenting racket that pushed everything else aside. Replacing conversation. Displacing thoughts. Irritating the imagination. He often didn't feel like emerging from his blanket cocoon in the back room of the safe house, even to visit with Lili.

Sleeping masked hunger too. The few hours allotted for shopping per week often turned up little or nothing. Neighbors squirreled away their acquired provisions, not willing to share. Occasionally when it was safe to be outside in the tiny yard, his father rigged up a hot plate over a campfire and "baked" a flat bread, *"langos"*, with flour and water, a treat that had to be consumed on the spot before anyone else noticed.

The safe house proved to be far from safe. Frequent air raids and false alarms kept residents inside as the Red Army advanced to the outskirts of Budapest, directing an intensive artillery and aerial bombardment against the German troops who were positioned around and within the city.

When Fritz wasn't sleeping or reading, he paced around the tiny apartment like a caged tiger. The shells and bombs came more frequently each day, shattering most of their windows. When electric power, cooking gas, and heat disappeared, he was thankful for the field kitchens Wallenberg and the Red Cross had set up to keep the ghetto fed.

Soon the apartments became uninhabitable and everyone moved to the shelter in the basement. Fritz joined the other disgruntled residents day and night on the concrete floor—bedding placed on the perimeter and chairs from upstairs in the center. When the candles ran out, Fritz created new ones by pouring the wax into jars and inserting a string. He wished the rest of the challenges could be figured out. Boredom and restlessness overwhelmed his senses. And frustration. Lili beside him but no privacy for conversation. Or for anything.

Finally in desperation, he and Lily had braved the bombings and snuck upstairs to the ruined apartment, brushing aside the shards of broken windows and chunks of assorted rubble. And the fear. And his mother's probing questions when they returned downstairs.

Each day the battle crept closer. The rattling gunfire and thumping of mortar shells multiplied. Fragments of neighboring bombed houses spattered their house. Sometimes peeks outside revealed Jews from surrounding safe houses being jerked through their front doors and marched to certain doom.

Today a Swedish embassy representative brought split pea gruel and the warning to stay inside and be extra vigilant about being seen or heard. He reported that transporting Jews out of Budapest was becoming less feasible as the Russians advanced closer and soon would be taking control of the city. The Hungarian Arrow Cross Nazis were going house to house, seizing Jews for quick disposal before the Russians arrived. They were being marched to the Danube and shot, their bodies dumped into the river. The possibility that the Nazis would attempt to individually kill each remaining Jew became a frightening possibility.

That afternoon, in his corner, Fritz closed his eyes, longing to shove these fears from his brain, and drifted off to sleep. Suddenly, he jerked awake. Something was wrong. It was quiet. Eerily silent. He joined Lili and his parents with the other fifteen residents in the center of the main room. Their questions bounced around. "Was this a temporary reprieve from the bombing? Were there Arrow Cross soldiers outside waiting to pounce? Or Russian soldiers?" The latter's reputation included accounts of their frequent looting, raping, and murdering. What should they do?

By the third day, tempers were flaring. There was no longer anything to eat. Fritz volunteered to scout for food, ignoring his mother's tearful protests and Lili's searching eyes. "It will be safer for me to go alone," Fritz said and exited before anyone could stop him.

Emerging from the apartment shelter, Fritz choked on the stench of smoke and decay filling the air. Destroyed buildings predominated although a few dwellings like his own stood proud and defiant. Debris and dead bodies littered the street. Stores were empty or demolished.

Fritz spotted a small crowd around the corner and ventured over to investigate. A horse, killed by shell fragments, lay on the pavement. People were butchering it right on the spot. Fritz swallowed the bile rising in his throat and pulled the Boy Scout knife from his pocket. A hunk of meat would fill hungry bellies. No one had to know where it came from.

Liberation

The continuing silence soothed nerves yet taunted them all with its uncertainty. Then one morning there was something different. People outside were chattering and cheering at the top of their lungs.

Lili poked her head out the doorway. In her bare feet and night clothes, she joined her excited neighbors in the street, tuning in to breathless dialogues. The Germans had withdrawn across the Danube. The hated Arrow Cross had fled with them. The Russians had taken over. They were liberated! Lili threw herself into the frenzy, hugging friends and strangers.

*****

By the next day, the initial exhilaration wore off.

Scarce food made for groaning bellies and irritated interactions. Lili and Fritz braved brief ventures into the chaotic streets searching for food, dodging the swarms of looters scavenging for valuables. Whatever the plunderers didn't carry off was wantonly scattered – thousands of rolls of exposed film, large bags of rock salt, slit open, thousands of shiny paper clips, gleaming among the refuse. Anarchy and senseless destruction reigned.

Bombings were still intermittent. The plentiful Russian soldiers arrived with a well-deserved reputation of cruelty. They were not focused on just finding Jews; they were happy to rape or rough-up anyone, helping themselves to plenty of their favorite items – leather jackets and watches.

Lili finally could visit her mother and aunt, a bittersweet reunion since not all the news filtering in was encouraging. No one had heard from Lili's male cousins, uncles, father or brother since they were dragged into the unknown. A long time ago.

Lili and Fritz tossed around ideas for their future. They didn't trust the Russians' methods or motives which were already getting oppressive. Food continued to be scarce. Lili could see Fritz's growing restlessness. So hard to make decisions in an upside down world.

As they wandered among the neighbors, foraging

for food and news, they heard various whispered plans among their friends and other younger people. The surrounding farm villages still had plentiful food. The fervent Zionists wanted to immigrate to Palestine to help start the new nation of Israel. Others were trying to get to Australia or the United States. Passage through the mountains of Switzerland promised freedom and opportunity. All the plans sounded exciting. And dangerous.

Lili liked the idea of Israel even though she wasn't particularly religious. As a child, she had convinced her parents to follow some Jewish traditions at home. Celebrating the Sabbath and the holidays brought her comfort for the few years her family cooperated. However, she could count on one hand the times she had been in a synagogue and knew little about her religion. But having now experienced the suffering and persecution her fellow Jews had suffered for thousands of years, Lili was convinced a Jewish homeland was essential. She had never believed in anything. This seemed a good place to start. The more passionate she got about this idea, the more reluctant Fritz was in response.

Fritz had an aunt and uncle in New York City who might sponsor them. To him, New York was a more practical place to find a career and begin their lives together. But first they should get married. And then they needed to get out of Hungary. Soon.

She and Fritz walked the ruined streets to the magistrate's office on the morning of February seventh and joined a line of other bedraggled couples waiting for their chance at the marriage registry. Couples took turns being witnesses for each other in the five-minute ceremony. Several hours later, Fritz and Lili returned to the safe house, officially married.

Lili had always dreamed of a romantic wedding day with a white lace bridal gown, pink roses intermingled with baby's breath, and a festive celebration with food and dancing. That February morning was unlike those dreams and yet the fulfillment of many of her hopes. The ones that mattered. She belonged to someone who would love and honor her forever. Never again would she feel unseen or insignificant.

Lili's mother had sold some jewelry on the Black Market and produced a wedding dinner of Lili's favorite – Paprika Chicken and *spaetzle* dumplings. Her mother and aunt watched the couple with delight as they relished the tiny chicken, never eating a bite themselves. Some other friends offered a room in their destroyed apartment for the honeymoon night.

The next morning, Lili and Fritz walked to the train station with full knapsacks and sad goodbyes to await a freight train for southern Austria where their Zionist friends were meeting and guides were said to be available. Here they would begin their long trip to attempted freedom. They were strong and young and in love. Together they could relish the adventure and conquer any challenges.

Where Are We Going?

With care, Vivien's father, Peter, placed the food he had been squirreling away for weeks into his large backpack – black pumpernickel bread, cheese, dried meat and fruit, lentil cakes, tin bottles of water. He added two blankets, some clothing and a few toiletries.

Vivien watched, brow furrowed. Her small knapsack was already stuffed with warm clothes and thankfully, Scruffy. But the dolls and books had to be left behind. She had placed them in a carton under her bed, pushed out of sight, along with her tears. Another portion of precious things left behind. She still didn't understand where they were going or why they had to leave.

She tried one more time, "Papa, why do we have to go? Are we trying to find Mama and Fredrick? How are we getting there?"

Peter weighed his words. He didn't want to frighten Vivien with the expected consequences of the Russian occupation for a Nazi officer. Their goal was to wipe out all Nazis with no mercy. "I was not allowed to have children in this apartment. But here you are. So yes, we shall look for Mama and Fredrick while we go for a gorgeous walk in the mountains. And look at this costume I found for our trip."

Peter pulled an olive green, padded Russian soldier's uniform out of the closet to show Vivien, and then rolled it, squeezing it into the backpack. It had cost him nearly a week's salary on the Black Market, but it insured some measure of safety once they finished the train ride out of Hungary and set off for the mountains to escape into Switzerland. He didn't show her his gun which he had tucked under the uniform. Or mention his Nazi uniform in a sack ready to be disposed of before they left.

Vivien nodded solemnly. She trusted her papa even if she had no idea what was happening.

TEN

Elmsburg, New York 1963

Knowing Hurts

Lili placed the dinner plates in the dishwasher, suppressing her brooding thoughts. This was Marta's job, but she didn't have the energy to hold her daughter accountable tonight. The new requirements for the Homel account had consumed all of Lili's minutes at work. Since she was late, the children had heated up leftovers and eaten alone. With a sigh she peeked into the refrigerator, searching for something for her own dinner. Nothing looked appealing. She also noticed the children had not made their lunches. Lili was too tired to do anything about that either. They could buy hot lunch tomorrow.

Retreating to her living room chair with an apple, she tried to ignore the taunting voices inside her head reiterating her failures. Learning the skills for her job as mortgage assistant at City Savings Bank, commuting the thirty minutes to White Plains, and handling all the household chores was proving to be more daunting than Lili had imagined. Single parenting was difficult. College plans were an abandoned dream after their separation. Instead of feeling fulfilled by having a career, she only felt exhausted, empty, discouraged, and lonely.

Fritz had kept his word about all the Thursday night dinners with the children. He provided the money for bills and treated her with respect and politeness. But that made him seem even more of a stranger. This was not the man she had loved with her whole being since she was 15 years old. Twenty years ago. A lifetime.

Worst of all, Lili had put little clues together and figured out Fritz was having an affair. Snippets of overheard phone conversations, unexplained entries in the checkbook, and unusual attention to his appearance, all pointed in one direction. When she confronted him with her theory, he didn't deny it. Or explain. Or apologize. But why would he throw away everything that had knit them together for these many years? How could he intentionally hurt the only person who had walked with him through so many hardships and victories? Dwelling on these questions wounded her afresh each day. A numb brain would be a welcome alternative, but that too often eluded her.

Lili headed upstairs for a goodnight hug with Larry. Short and upbeat. Afterwards, she hesitated at Marta's door. What would tonight's mood be? Sorrow and irritation seesawed in Marta with tenderness and compassion. Lili tried to be patient and supportive. Being fourteen wasn't easy under the best of circumstances. They had made sporadic progress on the family project. Perhaps Marta sensed how hard it was for Lili to relive the past right now. Adjusting her face into a carefree smile, Lili tapped on the door and went in. Marta was sitting on her bed writing furiously on a notepad. Tears were coursing down her face. "What's up?" Lili asked, holding back the desire to wipe away her daughter's tears. And her pain. Unaccustomed rage coursed through her. Fritz had no right to wound their daughter.

"I'm writing Dad a poem. You can read it if you want," Marta said.

Lili took a deep breath, marveling at the complexity of this woman-child. "That's OK. It's for your dad, not me. And I'm so sorry..."

Marta interrupted her, "You didn't do anything wrong, Mom. You don't have anything at all to be sorry for. Dad's just being a jerk."

"There are many things I could have done differently," Lili said, ever the optimist. "I'm not a perfect wife. Don't be angry at your father."

Marta sighed, "I just wish everything was the same as it used to be. Oh, and Mom, could you come talk to my class as part of the family project? People have so many questions about your story."

Lili was startled, "Me?" She didn't have chic Macy's clothes, a fashionable pixie hairdo, or the correct New York accent. And she didn't have a husband—a very shameful thing in Elmsburg in 1963.

Gut Punch

Fritz paced back and forth in the tiny living room of his apartment. He missed the spacious house in Elmsburg. He missed his rose bushes. He missed his children. He almost missed Lili. Almost, but not quite enough.

The affair with Amy, his secretary, had been short-lived by mutual agreement. For all her enjoyment of partying, Amy's real desire was for marriage and stability. Outside of the bedroom and the office, they had little, if anything, in common.

His new entanglement was more complicated. Belinda was the wife of an old friend, also a European immigrant. Their children were of similar ages, and the two families often enjoyed visits, holidays, and outings together. Belinda had no intentions of leaving her husband and children, yet she was controlled by the physical passions and thrill of an illicit affair– just like Fritz was. If this relationship was discovered, it would be very painful for both families. And yet, they continued on.

Fritz glanced at the clock. Time to pick up the children for their regular Thursday dinner. As he drove, he filed some questions and jokes away in his mind to fill the inevitable awkward silences. He did love his children, but how could he reconcile all the broken pieces and competing scenarios? Wasn't being true to himself the only way to live?

Both the children piled out of the house as soon as he pulled up to the curb. "Where shall we eat tonight?" Fritz asked with forced cheerfulness as they drove on White Plains Road.

"Howard Johnson's," Larry answered as he did almost every week. "I still have 19 flavors of ice cream left to try."

Marta scowled but had no other ideas to offer.

"Well, you can't beat their burgers," Fritz said as they arrived at the orange roofed restaurant and slid into their usual booth. He was surprised when Marta joined in the dinner conversation, discussing school, the upcoming Peter, Paul, and Mary concert, and the latest civil rights events. Both children seemed to be learning and thriving. Despite his absence.

Larry decided on butter pecan for tonight's ice cream dessert. Marta stuck with her favorite, vanilla.

While they were walking to the car, Marta handed

her dad a folded piece of paper. "I wrote you kind of a poem," she said," but don't read it now."

Fritz gave her a nervous smile, hugged both the children and placed the paper in his pants pocket where it seemed to burn against his leg as he drove them home. Dread outweighed anticipation.

When he was seated in the apartment's one cozy chair, his favorite Chopin etude playing on the record player, he pulled out the poem and read:

> *So many questions*
> *So few answers*
> *How can love turn to hate, or worse, in-*
> *difference?*
> *And how do I love two people who don't*
> *love each other?*
> *Why can't happy last?*
> *Will I ever feel complete again?*
> *My heart tries to whisper hope*
> *But it daily turns to ashes in my hand*
> *Why can't we forget about the past and*
> *start from today?*

The words punched Fritz in the gut and sliced through the months and years of lying and pretending. Shattered through all the layers of deception, revealing his heart. And the ugliness of what he was doing.

His tears were swift and unexpected. He had not cried for many, many years, and now he couldn't stop. All those stuffed emotions were unleashed in wrenching, intense sobs. Marta had hit the nail on the head except for one thing. Fritz knew without a doubt that he finally did have to look at his past—his marriage, his affairs, his selfishness—all the way back to that day on the mountain trail. And he needed to come to terms with it all.

Visitors

Vivien's classroom buzzed with more than the usual enthusiasm. This morning the first two parents were sharing parts of their heritage stories – Tom's father, Jim, and Marta's mother, Lili.

Jim, wearing his Air Force World War Two uniform, spoke first. He focused on his creased notecard, folding and refolding it, but when the students started peppering him with questions, he relaxed and entertained them with impromptu vignettes of his overseas experiences, such as the "bat bomb": a plan to attach time-delayed incendiary devices to bats who were placed inside bomb casings. When the bombs were dropped, the casings opened, and the bats dispersed, roosting in Japanese attics until the incendiaries ignited and set the wood houses on fire. The students focused on every word.

Vivien was surprised how little Marta resembled her mother. Lili was dressed in a simple beige sweater and a navy pencil skirt, one strand of pearls circling her neck. Her black hair was chin length and straight unlike Marta's brown, unruly waves. She addressed the class with calm poise as she told how the Nazi occupation changed her life from a carefree schoolgirl to a teenager desperately struggling for survival. Vivien noticed how nervous Marta appeared, eyeing the ground, but sometimes looking right at her mom with a proud grin.

Lili seemed to enjoy interacting with the students, answering their inquiries, adding extra details, and pointing out different locations on the wall map. However, Mary's question instantly changed the whole climate of the room. "How did you get out of from Hungary after the War?"

Vivien could see the walls come up. Lili's eyes shifted down, her body tensed, and her voice faltered, "That part will have to wait. I haven't even told Marta that story yet."

Vivien stood up, allowing her role as teacher to take over. "Thank you both so much. We appreciate you talking to us today, and we learned a lot of new information."

As the parents left, she turned to the class, "Let's write each person a thank you note. The proper format is on page 128 of your English book." Vivien avoided meeting Marta's eyes. She didn't want Marta to see her mother's response mirrored in Vivien's own face. Some chapters screamed pain and were better left closed.

The long postponed dinner with Annie was scheduled for tonight. They both harbored undisclosed chapters. Vivien's heart accelerated. Was it time?

That Poem

Marta dropped her thank you notes on Mrs. Harris's desk as the bell rang. "Your mother did a marvelous job," her teacher said, giving her an empathetic smile

"Thanks," Marta mumbled. She was surprised how confident her mom had sounded, not at all like the apologetic, mousy woman Marta was accustomed to. "And thank you for listening to me last week about my parents," Marta added. "I needed to talk to someone about what was going on with them, and I didn't know who else I could speak to."

"Did it help?" Mrs. Harris asked sympathetically. She had no experience or advice on divorce, but she did understand pain and sorrow. And Marta had wiggled her way into her heart.

"Yeah, I wrote my dad a poem about all my feelings and gave it to him last Thursday."

"Wonderful idea," Mrs. Harris said.

Marta nodded and headed to her next class. She hadn't expected a response from her dad, but she was still a bit disappointed to not have heard anything at all from him. It *was* kind of a weird poem, not like her rhyming one about music that had already been accepted for the yearbook's literary page.

Thursday and dinner with her dad were only two days away. And the more she thought about it, she wasn't sure if she wanted to know his reaction. Marta did love and respect him. So much. She didn't want to rock the boat any more than it was already rocking.

It's Time

Fritz stared at the black, shiny telephone perched on the end table, willing his hand to pick up the receiver. His mind and body felt disheveled from a week of sleepless nights. He had cancelled the Thursday dinner with the children, claiming a flu bug. And he did feel sick. From head to toe. No longer could he live with this person he had become. Fritz knew what he needed to do.

Dialing the familiar number, he broke out in a sweat. Scenes and sentences swirled around in his mind. At the sound of Lili's voice, his resolve strengthened. "We need to talk," he said in a calm voice, tinged with all the kindness he could muster.

Date Night

Lili's hands shook as she fastened the clasp of her favorite pearls around her neck. Glancing in the mirror, she smoothed down the blue silk blouse. New clothes were one benefit of her bank job. Along with advanced work skills and confidence. But as the shaking hands and fluttering in her stomach reminded her, she was tense and nervous about a "date" with Fritz. Even before this year's separation, it had been a long time since they'd enjoyed a special evening out with just the two of them. She did not want to get her hopes up about what tonight could signify. She didn't want Fritz to still have power over her. When Marta's eyes had sparkled at the news, she reminded her daughter too – this was only one dinner.

Hearing the children greet Fritz at the door, Lili walked down the stairs. Fritz was dressed up in a suit she didn't recall ever seeing but with the green tie he always wore for special occasions. His hair was curling behind his ears and at the collar, obviously in need of a haircut.

From the direct stare Fritz gave her, Lili felt he was perhaps observing her with fresh eyes. "So, where do you want to eat?" Fritz asked while they walked to his car. I am up for anything – except Howard Johnson's."

Lili forced a smile. "How about the Parkside? It's

quiet, and I don't believe there are hamburgers on the menu."

Once they were seated at a discreet corner table in the candlelit restaurant, both Fritz and Lili studied their menus with total concentration. The air was thick with tension. After they gave the waiter their order, Lili decided to plunge in. "I assume we have some business to take care of?" She was determined not to end up the victim in this conversation.

Fritz cleared his throat and looked right at her. "Lili, I am so sorry. I have made a total mess of everything, and I don't know how to fix it."

Lili was taken aback. She wasn't expecting those sincere words or the broken expression on Fritz's face. It had been so many years since he had expressed any regret or even weakness. About anything. She had been prepared for more rejection or excuses or angry reactions. Not this. She paused and took a deep breath. "What can I do?" she asked, wanting as usual to fix things.

"You haven't done anything wrong," he answered emphatically. "It's been me – not appreciating you or working on our marriage, and for making poor choices. Lots of poor choices. I hate who I've become. But it goes much further back."

Lili waited, knowing what was coming next, stomach twisting in knots.

"I have never dealt with what happened when we

were escaping from Budapest." He looked right into her eyes. "I think I am going to need professional help to sort it all out. But I want you to be part of the solution. Lili, I can't do it alone. I need you."

Lili shifted her gaze to the floor. She shouldn't capitulate so soon. Could her trust in Fritz be re-established? Did she want to walk on this path with him? Was she willing to give up her new-found independence and self-sufficiency?

The silence seemed to last for hours, but the decades of unconditional love within her won. She locked eyes with Fritz. "I will need time and space to work through my hurt. But I want to try and do this together, like we did in the past. It really is <u>our</u> story."

Without hesitation, Fritz reached over and squeezed her hand. "Yes it is, and a story worth redeeming."

Hope

Marta doodled on her notepad. She felt the twinges of a poem hatching in the corners of her mind. Happiness was starting to take shape. It was getting late though. The poem could wait till tomorrow.

She was almost asleep when the creaky front door jerked her to attentiveness. "Mom?" she called out from her opened bedroom door.

"What are you doing still awake?" her mom

scolded as she entered, stroking Marta's cheek who even more than usual had her feelings painted all over her face. Answering the unspoken query in Marta's eyes, she said, "Dad is moving back in. We are going to try and work things out."

Marta grinned at her mom. "Great. Now I can go back to being an obnoxious teenager!"

But they both saw hope in the other's eyes, overriding all the unanswered questions.

How Can You?

Marta strolled home from the school bus stop with an uncharacteristic contented smile. The sun was warm for early June. And there were only three days left of school. Today she received her English family history paper back with a big, red A+ circled on the upper corner. Topping that, Billy had stopped at her locker after Math class and talked for a few minutes, just the two of them.

As she unlocked the front door, she was surprised to see her mother at the kitchen table. "What are you doing home so early?" Marta asked.

"I had a dentist appointment at one, so I took the afternoon off," her mother answered. "Join me for a cup of tea? It's been a while since we had time for just the two of us."

"Sure," Marta said as she rummaged around in

the cupboard for her favorite cinnamon tea. "Guess what? I got an A+ on my family history paper."

"That's wonderful!" Her mother's eyes shone with pride. "I'm sorry we ran out of time to finish the story, but we will soon – both Dad and I."

"I included maps of different places in Austria and Hungary, and a timeline I found of the Holocaust. I used the few pictures you had and some others from magazines. Mrs. Harris told me the writing was outstanding," Marta said, bringing her teacup to the table. "I do want to hear what else happened," Marta added although she wasn't sure she did want to know.

Things seemed so strange with her dad here again. She could tell he was attempting to be nice to all of them. He wasn't as critical with her mom as before, but she still felt tension in the air. Especially when he was quiet. Sometimes his silence lasted for days. For Marta, that was almost worse than the harsh words.

"Mom, how could you forgive Dad? He moved out on us." Marta hadn't planned on saying that. The words leapt out from some hidden place deep inside her.

Her mother regarded her with unruffled eye "When you love someone, you try to forgive them if they wrong you. Dad is truly sorry. That doesn't mean I stop struggling with the memories and hurts. But I never stopped loving your dad. I can't <u>not</u> forgive him."

Marta sipped her tea, adding her mother's comment to the growing list of things she didn't understand.

Especially that one word.

Forgive.

My Dream

Hiding again behind his newspaper as the commuter train left the station, Fritz's mind kept circling through the same thoughts. How could he change his marriage? How could he change his emotions? How could he change his life? Big questions. Elusive answers.

The counselling sessions were productive. Lili attended the first few meetings, but now they were focusing on Fritz. He told his counselor everything he could remember about his past and his years of marriage. The counselor was helping Fritz gain valuable perspectives. But each new revelation unlocked more baggage and garbage. And more questions. His communication with Lili was improving somewhat, but not as much as he had hoped. Fritz felt stuck. The only clear idea taking shape in his mind was an unexpected one. As he worked through the counselling process, he felt a growing conviction that he was on the wrong career path.

Instead of managing a garment factory—the machines, the schedules, the unions, and the profit margins—he wanted to learn how to genuinely help people. People who were struggling like he was. The thought of pursuing a college degree was daunting but exhilarating. A dream abandoned long ago. What would Lili think? Perhaps tonight was the time to find out.

His Dream

The traffic ground to a halt on the expressway north. Lili frowned as she realized dinner would be late again. She should have prepared something ahead of time. Her job at City Savings Bank was interesting, and she was becoming more proficient in the various tasks. Her supervisor had even hinted at a possible promotion yesterday. But balancing her job and responsibilities at home was frustrating. She didn't like doing things halfway. Fritz and the children would help when asked but rarely with cheerfulness or attention to details.

Last night's conversation with Marta rattled around in her brain, bringing new painful questions. Yes, she had forgiven Fritz, repeatedly, sometimes every hour. She just wasn't sure she trusted him. His awful silences bothered her more than anything else. It made her feel invisible. She knew he was wrestling with himself. But in the process, he was shutting her out. Again. And that hurt.

Last night's discussion was somewhat unsettling but maybe offered a new road to hope. If he started night classes at college, it would complicate their family's present life, but he would be pursuing his dream for a more fulfilling career and perhaps, a happier life together.

At least one of them would have that opportunity. Lili tried to swallow the bitter resentment that managed to creep around every corner.

Condensed Version

Vivien looked up from her desk as Marta poked her head in the doorway. "I wanted to come by before summer vacation and tell you how much I appreciated all the encouragement you've given me this year. And thank you for recommending me for the Sophomore Honors Class. Will you be my teacher?"

"Well, I won't be teaching any classes next year." Vivien patted her stomach. "I am having a baby."

"Oh, that's great!" Marta responded. "Congratulations. But I will miss seeing you at school. I still do want to hear your Budapest story someday."

"And I want to hear the rest of your story, too. If you have a few minutes, I can give you a much abbreviated Reader's Digest version of mine, right now. I feel like I've put you off all year."

"Sure. My next class was cancelled because of finals," Marta said.

"OK. This is the condensed account. I can give you more details when you come over to meet the new baby." Vivien motioned for Marta to take a seat by her desk. "My father was a Nazi officer in Germany. We were stationed in Budapest when I was five years old. My mother and my brother disappeared when we were attempting an escape to Spain. I got left behind by accident."

Vivien shuffled some papers on her desk, tears still rising to her eyes after all these years. "When the Germans were defeated at the end of the war, my father took me out of Budapest because the Nazis were being hunted down. While we were escaping into the mountains, my father was captured or killed when he was searching for water to drink. He never came back for me."

Marta gasped, and Vivien met her incredulous stare.

With a deep breath, Vivien continued. "Some people found me beside the trail and took me to an orphanage in Switzerland. I lived in several foster homes waiting to be adopted. Most of them were fine though transitory. In the last one I was not treated well and ended up back in the orphanage. When I turned 18, a donor paid my way to go to the United States and attend teacher's college in New York City. I met my husband there, and – here I am!" Vivien cleared her throat and tried to loosen her tight shoulders. So much pain condensed into a few sentences.

Marta rubbed her brow, searching for the right words. "Wow, I don't know what to say." She shifted in her seat, lifting her gaze to Vivien's. "You had such a difficult life. And our stories are so – opposite. I have hated the Nazis all my life. I never even thought about their families and what they would have experienced. And then—you just happened to be my teacher. And you assigned me the discovery of my own family's story. You've given me a lot to chew on."

"Yes, there were many hard things," Vivien responded with a gentle sigh, "although my present life is certainly happy. And yes, it is amazing that our paths have intersected now. I trust this is all fulfilling a purpose in your life too." She walked to the doorway with Marta. "I hope your sophomore year is wonderful, and that you come to visit me in a few months."

Marta shook her head in affirmation and headed down the hall.

"Hey," Annie waved from the doorway a few minutes later. "Looks like you are making progress in packing up your classroom."

"It doesn't feel like it! Not even sure what half this stuff is. Come on in," Vivien responded. "I want to thank you again for everything. The projects and presentations exceeded my expectations. And my students' also. Your friendship means so much, and your life has inspired me."

Annie nodded, "I am going to miss talking and working with you. Can I be an honorary auntie, please?"

"Of course," Vivien hugged her. "Auntie number one."

"I've been meaning to ask you about something else," Annie said. "We've covered a lot of territory during our dinners, and I've alluded to this in our conversations, so I will spit it out. What do you think about church?"

Vivien raised her eyebrows in surprise. "I went to Mass every Sunday in Berlin and Budapest as a young child. It didn't seem particularly relevant then, and I guess I haven't thought about it since."

"Would you come with me sometime? The turning point in my life was seeing God as indeed relevant and involved in my past, present, and future."

Vivien tilted her head to the side, blinking. That kind of God almost sounded appealing.

ELEVEN

Eastern Hungary 1945

The Train

The irony of their situation brought a faint smile to Fritz's face. He and Lili had avoided being transported out of Hungary in a cattle car against their will for many months. But here they stood in the freight yard, knapsacks crammed with their most essential possessions, voluntarily searching for the right train to board to take them to Bludenz.

The cattle car they entered was packed with other young Hungarians, fleeing the Russians and the impending famine in the urban areas. They found a vacant spot on the crowded, dirty, metal floor to sit and leaned against their knapsacks, drifting between conversations. Each person had a traumatic story to tell and optimistic plans to discuss. Many agreed with what Fritz and Lili had already heard: get to the western Austrian border where there would be food to buy or trade and guides that could help them travel through the Alps to freedom in Switzerland. Several people confirmed that the Hungarian Zionist group was also gathering in the same town of Bludenz near the border to make plans for settling in the new nation of Israel. As the train left the station, the loud clanking ended most conversations.

The small slits near the top let air in, but without windows, there was no scenery to observe. Napping seemed the best option to pass the time, but the rough, rattling floors, frequent stops, and fussy children made sleep elusive. As the train again ground to a halt, Fritz sighed. At this rate, their ride would take weeks instead of days.

Suddenly Lili squeezed his hand. Tight. Five Russian soldiers had entered the open door. Using their pistols they motioned each young man onto the railway platform. No choice. No escape.

Fritz kissed Lili goodbye, leaving his knapsack, and promising to somehow meet her in Bludenz. He joined the other men on the platform of the deserted rural train station. Everyone had heard the rumors. The Russian army needed more soldiers. The camps in Siberia needed more workers. Any male would do – including young fathers with children or married men on their honeymoons. Panicked faces abounded, frustrated by their helplessness. So close to freedom. And now what? Again, Fritz needed a plan.

As the train departed, the soldiers marched the men in a loose formation through the countryside for kilometer after kilometer of corn fields bordered by sour cherry trees. Pretending to limp, Fritz started to fall back until he got to the end of his column which was guarded by a lone, very young Russian soldier.

"*Privyet,*" Fritz whispered, sliding up his sleeve to reveal his wristwatch which had not yet been "liberated." When the soldier's tired eyes lit up, Fritz handed it to him, pointing to the trees behind them. The soldier nodded. Fritz turned in that direction and ducked into some bushes. Another miraculous escape! This was almost enough to make him believe there was a God. But not quite.

Not So Alone

The cattle car filled with women and children, now felt more like a curse than a promise to Lili. What could she do? She had two very heavy knapsacks and no plan for her somewhat nebulous destination. Lili's usual bravado and optimism had disappeared along with Fritz.

Out of necessity, the young women who had been left behind allied together, sharing their limited food supplies and their more limited knowledge of how to proceed. They decided to travel to whatever destination they had already planned, hoping their husbands would maybe someday show up.

A few days later when their train ground to a final halt at the end of its line, Lili followed some of her new friends toward a different freight train that would get them to Bludenz. She crisscrossed multiple tracks, keeping a worrisome eye out for the oncoming trains. Weighed down by a knapsack on each shoulder, she started falling behind, straining to keep the other women in sight.

Lili was almost there when she heard the train whistle blowing. Desperately she ran faster, eyes on the women that were already boarding, and then tripped on the uneven ground. As her knee smashed on the gravel and the knapsacks slipped to the ground, her sobs poured out. So close. And so alone.

Someone tugged at her shoulder. Two of her fellow travelers had left their new cattle car and were carrying both knapsacks while dragging her to the closing door. Minutes after they shoved her, the knapsacks, and themselves in, railway workers slammed the door shut. The three women collapsed on the floor, crying together in relief. One step closer. And not so alone.

Movie Star

As Peter and Vivien approached the Budapest train

station, they could see the long platform was swarming with Russian soldiers. They appeared to be zeroing in on the men congregating there, comparing their papers with ones the soldiers held. Peter tightened his grip on Vivien's hand. These soldiers couldn't be looking for Jews anymore. They must be searching for Nazis. Or other young men to conscript.

"Let's walk this way," he whispered to Vivien, turning down a side street which traversed a small park. "We are going to play a game. A make- believe game. Wait right here. I need to use the toilet." He deposited Vivien on a bench beside a public bathroom. When he emerged a few minutes later, he wore the Russian soldier's uniform from his rucksack.

"Ready to pretend?" Peter tipped his daughter's chin to meet his tight smile. Vivien nodded, fixing serious eyes on him. "We both are going to have different names. I am Alexei Petrov, and you are Vladlena Lebedev. These are tricky to say, so let's practice."

After several attempts, Vivien mastered the pronunciation. "Do I wear a costume too?" she asked.

"No," Peter answered, "but you get a new story. You are my niece instead of my daughter. Your parents died in an air raid in Vienna last week, and I am taking you to Salzburg to stay with your grandparents."

Vivien parroted back the information to Peter's questions about her new identity several times, and they headed back to the train station.

"It's like being in a movie, "Vivien said, nervousness mixed with playful delight.

Peter smiled at her. "And you, my dear, are the star.

Horse in Time

Fritz shifted his cramped legs. Mulberry branches in the claustrophobic hiding place poked at him while his growling stomach reminded him of the absence of any food or water. His captors were now out of sight, but in all likelihood, other Russian soldiers lurked nearby.

Hoof beats punctuated the silence. As Fritz peered from behind the bushes, he saw a horse-drawn cart filled with hay, rattling along the bumpy dirt road. Trusting the innocent appearance, Fritz emerged onto the lane. "*Szia*", Fritz called out. The young peasant pulled on the reins, and the shaggy, weary-looking horse came to an abrupt stop.

"*Jo reggelt kivanok*," he replied.

Fritz grinned at the traditional Hungarian greeting.

He explained his plight to the farmer who introduced himself as Miskos. Having just retrieved his horse and cart from the Russian Army, Miskos was also travelling to Bludenz to his family's farm. He even had the necessary paperwork to assure safe passage, and some ragged blankets which could serve as a disguise for Fritz.

"Wrap the blankets around you, and tie this scarf around your head and your face too, if anyone gets close. You could pretend to be my mother," Miskos suggested, enthusiastic about the intrigue. "And just act like you can't understand Russian if we are stopped."

"That will be easy." Fritz smiled at his new friend. Here was a welcome solution. Miskos cleared a spot among the hay, handing him the blankets, scarf, and a chunk of bread.

The clumsy cart lumbered from village to countryside to village through flat, sparsely populated farmland. Each evening Miskos found kind farmers who sheltered them in barns and fed them with abundant food from the recent harvests. The few Russian patrols they encountered were satisfied with Miskos's papers and only gave Fritz a cursory glance. Dozing in haylofts each evening, with a full belly for the first time in months, Fritz wondered if he and Lili should change their plans and find their future as farmers in Western Hungary.

That idyllic bubble burst on their last night before reaching Bludenz. The amiable host at the farmhouse repeated the news he had overheard in the marketplace that morning. The new Hungarian government had declared war on Germany and was now actively conscripting an army to join the Russians in the final pursuit of German soldiers. The military draft was being introduced district by district, officers searching for all young, healthy men who hadn't been inducted by the Russians yet. Fritz had no desire to join the ragtag Hungarian Red Army.

Confirmation. Leave Hungary as soon as possible.

Arriving in Bludenz late the next day, Miskos left his passenger to continue on to his farm on the outskirts of town. Fritz thanked him profusely and set off in search of Lili.

Now What?

Lili swallowed the sting of disappointment, hopes dashed again as the last passengers emerged into the Bludenz train station. It was the sixth day she had been searching for Fritz among the incoming travelers. He was an expert at being clever and sneaky; he should have arrived by now if his efforts at escaping the Russian detachment were successful.

Eyes downcast, she plodded across town to the simple room in an abandoned school where she was staying with the Zionist group from Budapest. The broken windows were boarded up and bedding was distributed on the wooden floor. But the roof was intact and cheerfulness abounded.

Lili had been welcomed here and appreciated the warm companionship and the simple, communal food. She even found her friend, Vera, from her childhood neighborhood. But the constant talk of immigrating to Israel filled her with dread instead of the accustomed anticipation. There were many obstacles in the process which had become a political nightmare with no clear pathway. The paperwork was daunting. Diverse smaller groups competed for positions of priority. Israel was so far away. And so different. She couldn't imagine starting that new life without Fritz. She couldn't imagine any life without Fritz.

As Lili trudged through the doorway of the dark room, the chattering inside stopped. She could taste the silence. Before she could determine what was happening, a shadowy figure leapt from her mattress in the corner, enveloping her in a huge hug. "I found you!" Fritz exclaimed as everyone applauded.

For that week, the Zionist commune provided a welcomed respite for them. Here, life was almost normal: sufficient food, electricity, mail and radio service, even daily newspapers. Lili almost forgot about the multitude of unknowns: their families still dwelling under the oppression of Russian occupation. Or much worse.

As they all sat around the radio one evening, Lili gripped Fritz's hand in anguish as they listened to a broadcast from England describing the liberation of the Mauthausen concentration camp.

"Horrors beyond belief assailed our senses. The stench of rotten flesh permeated the air. Bone-thin corpses piled like firewood. Living skeletons, eyes vacant, too weak to speak, haunting imaginations forever."

The rumors were true. It was real. They had survived. But many millions had not. Including Lili's father?

Moans and weeping filled the whole room. Their fathers, mothers, brothers, sisters, grandparents, aunts, uncles, cousins. Whole branches of family trees, unreplaceable pieces of their heart. Gone.

It soon became obvious to Fritz and Lili that they didn't share the group's fervor for resettling in Israel or in their patience with the innumerable, shifting bureaucratic hurdles. Communal living sounded enticing during whispered conversation on the streets of Budapest as the nightmare of war was ending, but the present realities grated upon their nerves. They were never alone. Irritability reigned. Everyone rehashed every decision. They both felt suffocated.

Rumors of the approaching Hungarian military

draft increased. Russian soldiers were said to be everywhere, in Austria now as well as Hungary. It was time to move ahead with their own individual plan of escape, no matter how daunting the risk.

Vorarlberg, Austria

Vivien snuggled next to her father, watching the endless stream of picturesque farms and villages roll by the train window. She wasn't supposed to say anything in Hungarian or German. Her Russian vocabulary was limited to her new name, yes, no, and thank you. In the silence, thoughts of her mother and brother paraded through her mind. She missed them terribly. Were they alive? Would her father ever find them?

When the train pulled into the station at Vorarlberg, it was evening. Not being able to ask her father questions emphasized Vivien's confusion. Where were they? Could her mother and brother be here in this small town?

Her father led her down a few narrow blocks of cobblestone streets before arriving at an ancient slate building with a green sign proclaiming the availability of rooms for rent. Vivien smiled as she mouthed the understandable German words. The proprietor led them up narrow rickety stairs to a tiny room filled with a four posted bed and a mirrored dresser. After a quick snack from the knapsack and a change of clothes, her father tucked her under a feathery comforter. In minutes she was sound asleep.

Peter tossed and turned beside her, envying his daughter's apparent peace of mind. He wished he didn't know how difficult this next part would be.

Off We Go

The last few days had flown by like a whirlwind. After deciding to leave their Zionist companions, Fritz and Lili planned to walk the forty minutes to the little village at the base of the Ratikon Mountains which formed the border between Austria and Switzerland. Friends at the commune provided the name and location of a possible guide. Using their meager possessions, they bartered for better hiking shoes and other warm, suitable clothing. Sadly Lili took the remainder of the family jewelry from its hiding place in her jacket hem to sell for the necessary cash. She would miss these last tangible pieces of her past life.

When Fritz and Lili returned to the commune that morning after finishing their errands, they were met with complete chaos. "Hungarian soldiers just seized all the men here to conscript them and join with the Russian army in pursuing the Nazis," Vera sobbed. The whole room was full of distraught women, not a male to be seen. "They suspect some men were missing and promised to come back," she added.

This confirmed the decision. It was time for Lili and Fritz to depart and head to the village of Vorarlberg. A closely shaven Fritz would again dress as a woman, hoping to meet Pista, the recommended contact in the tavern there for the next part of their journey.

"How do I look?" Fritz asked an hour later after he donned his new disguise in a quiet corner of the city park. He twirled around in a blue pullover sweater and brown pleated skirt of Lili's.

"Quite ridiculous," Lili retorted. "Everything is too tight, and you look more like a clown than my mother."

"How about if I add my jacket and my stocking hat?" he questioned with a smirk.

"Passable if no one looks too close. Let's go," said Lili. Slinging their knapsacks over their shoulders, they set out for the unknown. Again.

Eight on a Bed

Trying to ignore the knot in her stomach, Lili reminded herself of what was important. They were together again. They had a plan. Everything was working out. But the same thought that haunted them both kept rising to the top. How many times could they overcome all the challenges that kept arising?

The sun shone with great intensity as they walked in silence along the country road, eyes always scanning the few people and vehicles they passed. If she didn't voice her doubts, Lili could squeeze them out of her mind.

Sweat was pouring down her face by the time they arrived in Vorarlberg later that afternoon. Poor Fritz was drenched in his many-layered costume. It was easy to spot the tavern with its gray gabled roof, outside wooden tables, and painted sign proclaiming *Bier* among the few buildings situated around a small town square.

"Do you think it's safe to take off your disguise now?" she asked Fritz. "Pista might be expecting a couple. This looks like too peaceful a place for any kind of soldiers."

He nodded, stepping into a nearby alley and stripped off the extra clothes, stuffing them into their knapsacks. As they entered the smoky tavern, the only customer rose and extended his hand. "*Halo*, I am Pista." Lili was taken aback by how young this man appeared. He couldn't be older than 18 with his ruddy cheeks, brown curls, and slight build. And how did he know they were looking for him?

As if reading her mind, Pista said, "This village is

the embarkation for travel through the Ratikon Mountains. The Russians haven't figured that out yet, the
Hungarian soldiers are too distracted, and the Nazis
are almost gone. So the few strangers who find their
way here come to find a mountain guide."

Fritz nodded. "Yes, that is our purpose. We were
sent by *Zionismus* of Budapest. We have the funds to
hire you."

Pista stood up and gestured to the door. "We will
start in the morning. Do you want to stay with my
family tonight?"

Lili and Fritz exchanged quizzical glances. They
really had no choice but to entrust themselves to this
young man. They grabbed their knapsacks and
squeezed next to him on the front seat of a gray, battered pickup truck parked in front of the tavern.

Several bumpy miles later, Pista pulled up to a
sprawling farm, complete with red barn, brown and
white cows, gray matted sheep, and cackling chickens,
all wandering around the yard. The tiny farmhouse,
constructed of rough-hewn stone and topped with a
thatched roof, looked centuries old.

As they stooped to enter the low door, they were
welcomed by the cool darkness and astonishing
smells of roasting meat, garlic, onion, and vegetables.
The bustling, rotund woman who introduced herself
as Pista's mother, motioned them to the abundant
feast of chicken, potatoes, fresh rolls, and three kinds

of vegetables spread on a rough plank table where the rest of the family had started eating.

Lili wondered if this was a dream. She hadn't seen so much food in years. Fritz's descriptions of his recent travels and farmhouse meals had seemed exaggerated, but here were piles of everything that could possibly be raised or grown on a farm.

Pista's father, younger brother and two sisters focused on their meal and didn't have much to say. No one asked Fritz or Lili any questions or seemed surprised by their presence. So Lili concentrated on the feast before her, relishing each tasty morsel with gratitude.

Gradually her eyes adjusted to the dim light. The cottage consisted of one room containing the kitchen where they were eating and a huge bed set against the opposite wall. After dinner the women put away food, washed the dishes, and swept the floor of compacted soil while the men headed outside to do evening chores.

Lili wondered what happened next. She didn't have to wonder long. Pista and his family retreated to a dusky corner, emerging in their night clothes. The six of them situated themselves on the enormous bed, sliding together. Pista pointed at the remaining space and beckoned to Lili and Fritz to join them.

They looked at each other and tried not to laugh as they climbed on to the crowded bed. Another new adventure!

Exciting Journey

The sunshine broke through Vivien's dreams. Startled awake, she pushed aside the feathery comforter, scanning the strange room for something familiar. Her father emerged from the bathroom, *"Guten Morgen,"* he said, kissing the top of her head.

"You changed costumes," Vivien responded in the familiar German, "and you smell delicious, like you always did in Berlin."

He chuckled. "I found some shaving lotion in there similar to what I used long ago in Berlin. I decided to put that uniform away for a while. We can also put away out pretend story. Let's pack up and find a bakery that smells even better than shaving lotion."

While tossing and turning that night, Peter had decided that looking like a Russian soldier would be too noticeable travelling through the Ratikon Mountains. And hopefully no one was questioning men and searching for escaping Nazis in this tiny, provincial village. Today he would be a local father taking his young daughter for a stroll in the nearby mountains. The Russian uniform would be useful later. And his officer's pistol, tucked next to it, might be even more essential.

"Where are we going today, Papa?" Vivien asked.

Peter gazed into her round, trusting eyes. How much should he tell her? Pulling a well-worn map from his jacket, he pointed to a small dot. "This is where we are now. We will be starting a long, thrilling hike right through these mountains." His finger traced a winding route on the map.

Vivien clapped in excitement. "What an adventure, Papa!"

Peter was thankful his innocent daughter had no idea what travelling alone on that twisting line entailed.

TWELVE

Elmsburg, New York July, 1963

Head Start

Humidity saturated the July day. Marta cradled the squirmy toddler on her lap, relishing the little boy smell of Timmy's black, curly hair. The children and aides perched on the red braided rug in the story corner of the large sunny classroom as the head teacher read aloud from a large Grimm's Fairytale book. Most of the kids focused on the dramatic words and colorful pictures, ignoring the few wiggle worms. Bins of toys lined the walls which were adorned with three- year-old art creations and posters about shapes, numbers, colors, and letters.

Timmy snuggled against her chest, surprising Marta anew with how much she enjoyed this summer job at Head Start, the government early childhood program for low-income children. It was her mother's dream to be a preschool teacher, not hers. Yet she had fallen in love with most of the children in this class. Making up silly stories and songs kept them focused, entertained, and content, something not all the other teenage aides were able to accomplish.

Many of the children from Greendale, were of different economic, social, and racial classes which Marta had never encountered in the lily-white, affluent town of Elmsburg where she had spent her entire life. Marta hoped she was making a difference for these children, giving them various tools to prepare for academic success as well as plenty of hugs. But just as often, she felt enriched by the unconditional affection given to her and glimpses of a whole different culture they represented.

A job gave her pocket money and kept her from focusing too much on the things she couldn't change about her own life. Marta was continually aware of what a misfit she was. Her clothes weren't stylish. She wasn't popular. She didn't have a group to hang out with. Classical music was more appealing than rock and roll. Television was not her favorite entertainment. And she must be the only one at school with such a messed-up family.

Marta jolted back to the moment as the story ended with the satisfying, "And they all lived happily ever after." Timmy wiggled out of her lap, heading to the truck bin.

"Hey, buddy", Marta said, one hand grabbing him and the other hand catching his friend, Tasha. "It's time to wash up for lunch. And today it's every-one's favorite—macaroni and cheese." They both grinned at her and dashed to the sinks. She was al-ways surprised when the children listened to her. It was lovely to be the boss of someone.

Conundrums

As the train jerked to another stop, Fritz's head snapped forward, and his notebook slid to the floor. Asleep again. How was he ever going to finish his homework before tonight's class at this rate?

His current plan was proving to be difficult to ac-complish. Working all day and then taking 12 credits of evening college classes left him with little time or energy for anything else. The assigned pages to read and reports to write swam around his brain without leaving any concrete evidence of the energy he ex-pended. He hated not doing things with excellence. But the load seemed impossible.

Fritz thought maybe things were better with Lili, but he honestly hadn't bothered to ask her. She was still working long hours at the bank. When they were both home, they were tired and preoccupied, ships passing in the night, not much conversation or affec-tion. Maybe he did need to follow through with more individual counseling.

Marta and Larry were so engrossed with their own lives, they seemed like strangers. Tennis now consumed Larry, and he no longer was interested in talking about baseball. Marta wasn't interested in talking, period.

And then there was that perky brunette in his Sociology class who was always asking him questions. She managed to find a seat next to him on most evenings. And he was upset to find himself wanting to respond to some of her flirtations. Wasn't he past those kind of temptations?

Lili had reminded him several times of the promise to Marta about finishing their life story. Another conundrum. Did Marta really want to know? Did he want to tell her?

Dreams

Lili stirred the pot of *Szeky* goulash, swirling a finger through the cubed pork, sauerkraut, and rich broth for a taste. Perfect. All that was needed now was someone to eat it. On cue, the front door slammed shut, and Larry yelled his customary, "Yum!"

"Take off your shoes, and wash up for dinner," Lili responded, knowing a day of yardwork would have left a load of sweat and dirt all over Larry.

"Hey, mom. I've got a tennis match at seven. Can

we eat soon?" Larry asked.

"Marta should be home from Head Start any minute. Dad's train comes in at 5:45, so dinner at 6:15 should work," Lili said. She sighed. Trying to keep everyone's schedule straight was almost as complicated as making everyone happy. And just as frustrating.

She flipped on the radio to her favorite station, WQXR. The familiar strains of a Mozart horn concerto worked its calming magic on her as she set the table for dinner. When the orchestra finished with a final flourish, the announcer came on. "This station will now bring you the highlights of Dr. Martin Luther King's 'I have a Dream' speech given today during the March on Washington."

Lili grimaced. Her dreams of finishing college and becoming a teacher or someone of significance would not be broadcast. But they continued to live on inside her.

Baby Coming

Nestled in the recliner, Vivien startled as she felt that tiny foot pushing inside her huge belly again. This baby seemed determined to kick its way out into the world. Well, Vivien was more than ready. Everything in the nursery was perfect – pastel yellow walls freshly painted, tiny fuzzy sleepers folded in a pile,

Mother Goose mobile and teddy bear paintings in place.

Yesterday's doctor's visit was disappointing though. After the thorough exam, Doctor Miller pronounced his verdict, "Looks like you are having a baby! But maybe not for a few more weeks. Remember – due dates are only an educated guess. Enjoy your last nights of uninterrupted sleep."

"Spoken just like a man," Vivien thought. No position in bed was comfortable, no matter how many pillows she tried in various positions. And the bathroom beckoned relentlessly throughout the night.

Paul slept on the couch to allow for all her tossing and turning. His cheerful teasing and encouragement did help calm her nervousness and fears. She knew she was a skilled teacher, but what did she know about becoming a parent? For the umpteenth time she wished she had a photograph, a letter, something to clarify or anchor the fuzzy, fading memories of her mother.

If only the memories of the last days with her father and the disastrous foster homes would fade away as effectively.

The doorbell provided welcome relief to her disturbing thoughts. Vivien waddled to the door, grimacing as the baby shifted against her tailbone.

Annie stood on the top step with a huge smile, thrusting an enormous teddy bear toward her friend.

"Number one auntie here, wanting to say goodbye to this dear pregnant belly."

Vivien beckoned her in. "Thanks for interrupting my pity party! This teddy bear will be perfect for the corner by the crib. And I'm ready to say goodbye to this pregnant belly as well. Tea?"

"Sure." Annie followed her to the kitchen and perched on a stool. "I have something for you also – reading material for all those leisurely days ahead." She pulled a few paperbacks from her roomy purse. "These are by my favorite author, C.S. Lewis. He was instrumental in helping me explore and understand some of my intellectual grappling with the Christian faith."

"Thank you. Grappling does describe my journey right now. I enjoy going to church with you. The music is amazing and the people so welcoming. I just can't get the puzzle pieces to fit together. Suffering, pain, war, human choice…"

"Well, you are not alone in that." Annie grinned. "Twenty centuries full of similar questions. It will take time. Please be patient. All the questions might not be answered, but there *is* a peace that passes all understanding. I pray for that every day for you." Annie squeezed her hand. "And you'll have to let me know how Janelle, the counselor I recommended, works out."

Vivien leaned over to attempt a hug. "I am so

grateful for you. And look," she placed Annie's hand on a rippling section of her gigantic belly, "so is Pip-squeak!"

THIRTEEN

Western Austria 1945

Next Step

To Fritz's surprise he slept through the night in the midst of the crowd in Pista's Vorarlberg farm house. By the time he opened his eyes, sunshine had poked through the one dusty window. Seven people had risen without disturbing him. Now the bed was blissfully empty. The pungent smell of frying sausage triggered thoughts of idyllic childhood mornings. Emerging from the covers he stood up, watching Lili bustle around the tiny kitchen, helping prepare breakfast, chattering away like she was part of the family.

They all squeezed around the plank table, again loaded with hefty quantities of various foods. After feasting on farm-raised sausage, ham, eggs, tomatoes, cheese, and bread, Fritz and Lili thanked Pista's family for their hospitality. Exchanging hugs, they bid them farewell and piled into Pista's pickup for the short ride to town, punctuated by the bumps on the road and Pista's cheerful chatter.

As they pulled into town, Fritz noticed a small group waiting outside the tavern. "Are you taking other people along with us?" he asked Pista with apprehension. Nothing of this had been mentioned last night. "I thought we paid for a private guide."

"Oh no. The more the merrier," Pista answered. "You can all watch out for each other and make lots of new friends."

Fritz wrinkled his brow, face clouding. He didn't want to watch out for other people. He didn't want other people to watch out for him. He didn't want any new friends. Tamping down the questions and the fear, Fritz offered a curt nod. Lili needed him to be brave. And he needed to trust Pista because there was no one else to trust. And no other options.

Not Fine

Lili followed Fritz as Pista gathered the group which had now grown to ten people, all around Fritz and Lili's age, to give instructions. "Dress in layers. It will be cold soon. Take only what you can carry on your back. Make sure you have enough food and water for several days. Stay close together. The trail can be rough, and we will cover many kilometers a day."

The carefree teenager had transformed into a serious, brusque guide. He answered a few questions and pointed towards a small store on the corner where they could obtain last minute provisions. They all focused on arranging their backpacks with little chatter, Pista's soberness casting a shadow over their excitement, the reality of danger coloring their enthusiasm. What had this quaint hamlet observed over the centuries as it nestled on the mountain border?

Within an hour they were on a trail that meandered out from the edge of town. The air was crisp and sunny, and the mountain ahead of them towered majestically. Lili had to remind herself this was not just another recreational outing with friends. Or was that a valuable pretense?

She was grateful for the sturdy hiking shoes she had purchased. The path soon got rocky and steep, and the pace was brisk. "How are you doing, *Schätzi*?" Fritz asked, coming alongside of her. His eyes were gleaming, and it was obvious he was relishing again being in the mountains, immersed in an adventure, peril and caution forgotten for the moment.

Lili smiled and lifted her face for a quick kiss. But not fast enough to notice the rock in front of her. She tripped. Her heavy pack intensified the fall as she thumped awkwardly to the ground.

Lili swallowed a groan. "I'm fine," she insisted as she scrambled to her feet, giving Fritz a reassuring nod. "We don't want to get behind the others." But she had felt something crunch in her ankle. She knew she was not fine.

Pleasant Outing

Peter squeezed Vivien's hand as she skipped beside him. He inhaled deeply, filling his lungs with the fresh alpine air. The beauty and the sunshine calmed his jangled nerves. Childhood memories of mountain vacations with his family flooded his mind, and he felt his body relaxing from the inside out. The information and the warnings he had collected about this journey faded into the background. A pleasant father-daughter outing indeed.

When they rounded a corner, Peter was surprised to hear the chatter of voices ahead of them. Somehow he had failed to envision sharing this trail with anyone. He couldn't distinguish the language at this distance. Rubbing the back of his neck, he nervously reviewed his options, deciding the Russian uniform might be the best disguise to appease Nazi-hunters or rambunctious civilians.

"Vivien, we are going back to our other game. I will put on my uniform and be a Russian soldier. You will be my niece. We'll rehearse your Russian words, but this time we will add something exciting. If we hear any other people, you must try to hide from them off the trail before they can spot you. Let's practice." Vivien bobbed her head with enthusiasm, and they had a brief game of hide and seek. Confident that Vivien could respond if someone appeared, Peter found a nearby bush to duck behind and change his clothes. He made sure the pistol was loaded and placed in the holster on the belt of his uniform.

By the time they started back on the trail, the only sounds his ears could discern were the chirping of birds and gurgling of a nearby stream. He sighed in relief, taking Vivien's hand again, striding along the wooded trail as the late afternoon sunlight filtered through the leaves.

Just Fine?

Beads of sweat glistened on Lili's brow. She clenched her teeth to hold back the whimpers that kept trying to escape. The pain threatened to swallow her. And all hope for the future. Her ankle kept swelling. Each step was like a vise squeezing her nerves. Fritz found her a sturdy branch for a walking stick which helped a bit. He tried to use another stick and a scarf as a splint but that added more pain. She had to act brave even though her body wanted to give up.

Around a bend, she spotted their group settled by a rushing stream and breathed a sigh of relief. Joining her companions with a brusque nod, Lili untied her shoe and peeled back the sock. Her ankle was fiery red and grotesquely swollen. Fritz helped position her on a flat rock by the creek so that she could place her foot into the icy water as they ate some lunch. The others chattered away without acknowledging her injury. Weakness was ignored; it would only spread fear and doubt.

Lili pasted on a tense smile and tried to join the conversation. It wasn't working. The throbbing was invading all her thoughts. When the others rose and prepared to resume their journey, she motioned Fritz aside. "What are we going to do?" Lili questioned in a panicked whisper. "I don't think I can keep up this pace. It hurts. Bad"

Fritz kissed the top of her head. "I'll talk to Pista. We will work something out. It will be just fine." He sounded much more optimistic than he felt. They did not have a lot of alternatives.

On the Trail

Fritz pocketed the austere map Pista had sketched for him. "Pista told me we should keep up with the group for as long as possible. If this becomes unmanageable, we have the map, and our common sense to guide us. He also contributed some rolls and cheese in case our journey got extended."

One of the women, a former nurse, examined

Lili's ankle and pronounced it a bad sprain rather than a break. "Don't wrap it if it's still swelling. The best treatment is to avoid using it," she said, "but I don't think even your handsome husband could carry you up this mountain." She patted Lili's shoulder in encouragement, but her face reflected the impossibility of the situation.

The next section of the trail was somewhat level and smooth. The cold water had reduced the ankle's swelling, and Lili almost mastered the walking stick. But as the path climbed the mountain and got rougher and steeper, it became obvious they wouldn't be able to maintain the rapid pace of the group. Fritz didn't know how to voice this new reality aloud.

"Fritz, I have to stop and rest," Lili interrupted his anxious thoughts. Fatigue and pain clouded her face. The quiet chatter of their group could no longer be heard.

"Here, let's turn off the path and find a sheltered place for you to sit. It's a bit hilly, but I think you can do it. I'm going to scout ahead and see if I can find the easier trail this map seems to show. It is probably a wise idea to stay hidden in the brush. We have no idea who else might be travelling on this path."

Lili nodded wearily and climbed off the trail behind some bushes, leaning against a large log and propping her ankle on her knapsack. "Just be careful, Fritz." Her smile was more of a grimace. "And watch out for the big, bad wolf."

Fritz met her eyes, stroking her arm. "Just rest, *Schätzi*. And trust me."

*****

Vivien was no longer skipping beside her father but shuffling like a wilted puppy. "Papa," she mumbled, "I am so tired. Can we rest now? And I'm thirsty enough to drink an entire lake."

Peter nodded, and they turned off onto a shaded area beside the trail. "Sit here, hidden behind this bush, and I'll give you some water." Pulling the canteen out of the side pocket of the knapsack, he observed with alarm that it was empty. Not a drop remained. The knapsack felt damp. The top of the canteen must not have been secured tightly.

"Vivien, I am going to find that creek we heard earlier and fill up the canteen. You must stay right here hidden until I return. No noises, please." Peter said with gentle sternness. He handed her their last half a roll to eat.

He stepped onto the trail without a sound, straining to hear the rippling of the stream. He was concentrating so intently on listening, he didn't notice the young man on the path ahead of him until he was only a few meters away.

*****

As he walked, Fritz focused all his attention on Pista's wrinkled map. Looking up to check a landmark, he was startled when a Russian soldier appeared directly on the path in front of him.

"*Octahobka*," Peter growled, pointing his pistol straight at Fritz's heart.

Fritz raised his hands in surrender. "*Da, ser.*"

Was this it?

*****

What were those noises? Lili propped herself up on her elbows from her hiding place in the bushes, attentively listening. She was sure she recognized Fritz's voice. She was almost as certain he had been speaking Russian.

Trying to protect her throbbing ankle, she crept with care the short distance to a small cliff that overlooked the trail below her. Sure enough, there was Fritz with his hands in the air. And a Russian soldier. Pointing a gun right at his heart.

What could she do? Lili squeezed her eyes shut in panic. And prayer. Opening her eyes, she noticed some boulders along the cliff. Was there one she could dislodge? With all her strength, swollen ankle screaming, she shoved a huge rock from the edge toward the Russian soldier.

Miraculously it slid down the mossy slope, accelerating as it rolled and clattered right behind the soldier. She saw him stumble, falling to the ground with a thud. She closed her eyes again in silent entreaty. And then she heard a shot.

*****

Fritz stood shaking, the pistol clutched in his trembling hands. What had he done?

The answer was in front of him. The Russian soldier was splayed on the ground, blood pouring from the center of his chest.

Fritz dropped to his knees, stomach lurching, body shuddering, willing himself to stare right at the face of this human being whose life he had just snuffed out.

*****

"Fritz," Lili hissed. He stood on the trail, stricken and unmoving. She limped to a spot where she could carefully lower herself next to him, landing on her good foot, forcing her gaze on his horrified face.

"What have I done?" he moaned, voice broken with anguish, eyes fixed in horror at the limp, bloody body in front of him.

"You did what had to be done. You shot him before he shot you. And now we need to finish taking care of things," she said, "Let's move this body immediately, before anyone comes along the trail."

As if in a trance, Fritz grabbed the soldier's shoulder while Lili took the feet, limping painfully. They managed to shove the heavy corpse into some nearby brush without getting blood on their clothes.

"What about the gun?" Lili asked.

Fritz's whole body shuddered, "I've always detested guns. I don't ever want to touch another one."

Using her sleeve, Lili cautiously picked up the pistol, wiped the handle, and placed it near the soldier. "Let's get to that stream and clean the blood off our hands. And then we better start walking—as fast as possible—no matter how sore my ankle is."

This was her turn to be courageous. But could she do it?

*****

Vivien ate the half a roll, letting each bite sit in her mouth until it dissolved. She closed her eyes, soaking up the sunshine. The birds were warbling all around her. She recognized the distinctive trill of a finch. The trees had the rich pine smell of Christmas. It was a beautiful spot. It reminded her of summer vacations outside Berlin on Lake Tagel when she was very little, her father teaching her how to swim in the chilly water. But where was her father now? And was that a clap of thunder she had heard?

As the sunlight started ebbing away, she jogged in a small circle around her spot, trying to stay warm.

Her mind kept rushing back to that other time, not so long ago on their attempted escape to Spain, when her mother and brother disappeared. "It couldn't happen again. Papa is so brave and strong," she kept telling herself. But still, the panic threatened to wash over her.

The unfamiliar night noises tiptoed closer as the darkness crept in. Soon the stars wheeled diamond-silent overhead.

"I must get near the trail, so Papa can find me in the dark," Vivien thought as she picked her way back to the path. And once again she curled up into a tight ball. Numb and beyond fear. Alone.

Never the Same

Fritz's mind was still reeling. Nothing in all his adventures or drive for excitement had prepared him for that decisive moment. Or for the irrevocable violence. But Lili was right; it was done, and they had to move forward. He willed himself to again be present, physically and emotionally for Lili. He was the strong, gallant hero, wasn't he?

The stream was close. The frigid water cleansed the blood from his hands and some of the torment from his mind. He and Lili were both alive. Freedom and safety were hopefully within reach.

After fetching their knapsacks and eating a few

hurried handfuls of their dwindling rations, they set off again, Lili leaning on her walking stick and sometimes on her husband. The beauty of their surroundings contrasted with the fear and anguish remaining in their minds.

"Lili," Fritz exclaimed within the hour, "here is the other trail I was looking for." Hidden in the thick foliage was a smooth, wider path arcing away into the woods.

"I wonder why more people don't use this one. It appears to be much easier," Lili mused.

"Pista said there isn't any water, and most outsiders don't even know about it," Fritz said. "But if we can keep up this pace, there's a slight chance we can meet up with our group when this branch intersects the main trail again. Or with someone else."

Lili shuddered, "I'd rather travel alone."

They continued in silence, Lili struggling to find a rhythm that didn't pressure her ankle, and Fritz struggling to lock all his disturbing thoughts into an isolated corner of his brain. The smooth path allowed them to make admirable progress even as darkness crept in.

When they started to have trouble seeing where their feet were going,

a very full and bright moon made its appearance. Fritz knew the rainbow had been a sign of God's promise for the ancient Israelites, but he had a strong hunch that this moon was a personal promise for them at this moment. From God?

It must be so. Within a few hours, they rejoined the main trail and heard voices ahead of them – voices they recognized.

Fritz felt close to weeping for the first time on this journey. He hugged

Lili close. "It's our group. We can try to keep up with them again. But say absolutely nothing about what happened. Lili nodded, locking her eyes to Fritz's serious ones. Their lives would never be quite the same. It was their own private nightmare.

Rescued Again

Bright moonlight awakened Vivien. Shivering, she wrapped her arms tighter around her body, willing those delightful dreams to recapture her mind. She fell asleep, rousing again to the sound of distant voices. Was it Papa? Should she go back to the spot where he had ordered her to stay?

Before she could decide, two shadowy figures came into view. And even from this distance, she could tell neither of them was her father. From their exclamations, she knew they had already spotted her. Or the little ball that she was now, folding more deeply into the foliage.

"Why, look what's here," a low gruff voice spoke

in German, "a little girl. Are you lost?"

Vivien poked her head up. In front of her was a man, much older and thinner than her father and a young woman with kind, gentle eyes. What should she do?

In response, the young woman, Gisella, gathered Vivien into her arms. "Markos, she is so cold. Let's stop for the night and stay with her. Are you hungry, *Mein Kliener*?"

Vivien nodded. "I am waiting for my father to come back from the creek. We are going to Switzerland." Gisella and Markos exchanged concerned looks over the top of her head.

"If he doesn't come by morning, we will take you with us to find him," Gisella said. "Meanwhile, look at all this delicious food we have. And warm blankets too. We will have a special campout."

Vivien squeezed back the tears. And the fear. She had no choice. Her life was put into someone else's hands. Again.

Maybe tomorrow or the tomorrow after, she would find her own people - to belong to forever.

FOURTEEN

Elmsburg, New York 1966

New Challenge

Fritz slammed on the brakes as traffic again ground to a halt on the Westchester Expressway. There was a solid line of cars ahead as far as he could see. He sighed and fiddled with the radio dial. In some ways he missed the commuter train days of effortless travel, newspaper in hand, dozing as picturesque, suburban towns rolled by.

That was the only thing Fritz missed. His counselling job at County Family Services was as challenging and rewarding as he had hoped. The staff was close-knit and supportive. He had a knack for drawing clients out and zeroing in on ways to help families connect with each other and relate in healthier ways. His own personal failures increased his compassion and insight. Fritz recognized his success in his gut. Feed-

back from the staff and his clients confirmed this opin-
ion, and his assurance that he had found his niche.

Flashing lights accompanied by harsh sirens confirmed an extended wait in traffic. Fritz's mind drifted
to his last Thursday's therapy session with Dr. Manning, the culmination of six months of probing, retreating, plowing deep. This man was an expert – experienced, compassionate, and relentless. Just what
Fritz had needed.

"Fritz, I don't think you are being honest with me or
yourself. Are your guilty feelings coming from killing
a soldier in an act of self-protection in the chaotic fog
of intense fear and danger? You made a choice to fire
a gun, and a death occurred." Dr. Manning's gaze was
unwavering.

"I don't know, Fritz sighed. "I have always des-
pised guns and violence. And he was not just a soldier;
he was also a person."

"But look what Nazi soldiers did to your people,
not considering their humanness at all," he responded.

"My family and I were spared so much of that. I
was an adventurous, daring teenager. Even when I
faced dangers I was wrapped in some sort of protective cocoon. But my cousins. My aunts and uncles. My
friends ..." It suddenly torpedoed Fritz. "I don't know
why I survived and avoided so much suffering and

horridness. And literally got away with murder. It's not fair. It's not right." He clamped his jaw tight and the intense, silent sobs shook his body.

Dr. Manning waited, eying him with patience. "It's called Survivor's Guilt, and Fritz, it's quite normal. Recognizing this is an important step towards healing."

Fritz took a long, shuddering breath. "That might be so, but the way I have treated my wife is inexcusable. As a child, I became the center of my parent's universe. I was charming and learned to manipulate people and situations. Our household maid was even made available to me for unlimited sexual 'education.' I can't blame all that on the war."

"No," Dr. Manning agreed, "You can't. Now you have a diagnosis for some of your problems. Learning to change your habit patterns and relationships will start after you are able to forgive yourself. That too is a process, but a very necessary one."

Tonight would be another step as Fritz presented some difficult topics together with Lili to Marta and Larry. His supervisor, Doctor Hayes, thought it essential for Fritz's family to participate in a counselling session together in order to model for Fritz what it felt like on the other side of the couch. And also to complete the chapter he and Lili had been reluctant to broach with the children.

Fritz and Lili had been silent for too long. Marta and Larry were in high school now, busy with their own activities and mature enough to hear the whole truth which had been festering within their parents for many years. But how much did he want to tell them? How much did they really want to know?

Time for Truth

Dr. Hayes' counselling office was air-conditioned, but Lili's armpits of her purple silk blouse were damp and clammy. She adjusted the lapels of the gray suit jacket and cleared her throat. Nervous would be an understatement. Could the children handle this? What would they think of their parents when they finally heard the whole truth?

Marta and Larry kept fidgeting in the straight-backed chairs, eyes fixed on the flowered carpet, probably more embarrassed than anything else. Or annoyed to be here instead of hanging around after school with their friends.

Dr. Hayes finished straightening the piles of papers on his desk and gave Lili a reassuring smile. This man had done incredible things for her and Fritz's relationship; his wisdom and insights brought them from the precipice of hopelessness to some semblance of a healthier marriage. Plenty of work remained, but they were now committed to doing it together.

Fritz looked uncharacteristically edgy, eyes shifting around the room, clenching and unclenching his fingers over the top of his tapping knee. They were sitting too far apart for her to grab his hand, and she didn't know if those old gestures of affection were still welcomed.

Dr. Hayes began by greeting them and explaining why this session was an important step for them as a family. "Marta and Larry, you know there has been a lot going on with your parents the last few years. Do you have any questions you would like to ask before we start?"

Both children still focused their eyes on the floor. Marta had emerged from an outspoken, sulky adolescent to a more reticent, but poised, young lady. Larry still didn't know how to handle emotional matters, preferring perpetual action to deep conversation.

"No sir," Marta said, and Larry nodded in agreement.

"Well, your parents do have some more things to tell you about their relationship and also about their past," Dr. Hayes said. "They think you both are grown-up enough now to know the whole truth."

The tension in the air could be sliced. Why had any of them ever agreed to have this meeting?

Lili took a breath, but thankfully Fritz plunged in. It was his story more than hers, and she would only have sugar-coated the details, attempting to make it all palatable for everyone.

"A few years ago, I was unfaithful to your mother on more than one occasion. It was wrong. It was stupid. I am so very sorry for the way I hurt her and damaged our family." The brief words spoke volumes. Had they suspected something? It didn't appear so. Shock and surprise were etched on Marta and Larry's face.

Lili looked searchingly at each of them. Marta seemed frozen in distress. Larry glared, lips flattened.

"You might have known some of this," Fritz continued, eyes overflowing with pain. "I want to put everything out in the open and ask for your forgiveness, so we can all work on healing, as a family and as individuals. I know it will be a lengthy process, and I understand if you need more time for questions and to think about things." Fritz paused. The weight of hurt and pain settled in the silence around them.

He focused on each of them in turn. Larry met his eyes and dipped his head. Marta burst out in fury, "Dad, how could you?"

"Marta, can you voice what you are feeling now?" Dr. Hayes asked.

"My dad was my hero. I always looked up to him. It bothered me when he spoke unkindly to my mom, but I never dreamed he'd do something…"

Marta paused, wringing her fingers, "something terrible like this. I don't know if I can ever forgive him." She pressed her fist against her mouth as she held in any further response, refusing to look at either of her parents.

Dr. Hayes spoke with measured calmness. "Marta, forgiveness does not mean that you are letting anyone off the hook for what they did. Or that you can forget. It is a deliberate choice to release your hurt or resentment or anger towards someone, regardless of whether they deserve to be forgiven. Your dad is wrestling with sincere guilt and shame. You have to choose how you will react."

Lili walked over to her daughter, laying a gentle hand on her shoulder. "I have forgiven your dad. We are working hard on putting our marriage back together. It's difficult work, and it will take a lot more time and help, but we are dedicated to doing it. I hope in time you and Larry can also."

Dr. Hayes nodded in agreement. "Forgiveness is a difficult but essential journey – for you and for your dad. We can all continue to work together on it. And now, are you all ready for more?"

No one looked enthusiastic about this question. In fact both the children looked horrified at the idea of more.

"I'll start," Fritz said. "Marta, because of your family history project, we have told you a lot of our family stories from Vienna and Budapest during the

War and how our situation afterwards kept deteriorating. Larry, I don't know how much you know or are interested in, but there is one last chapter we do need to share."

Marta stared straight at him, face cold, hands knotted on her lap. Larry's eyes locked on some crumbs on the carpet.

"When we decided it was time to leave Budapest, we didn't have a lot of options. There were no exit visas being given, and we didn't have the money to arrange things on the black market. Young men were being conscripted as soldiers by the Russians and the Hungarians where death was the likely end. Food was running out all over the city. My parents and Lili's mom could barely take care of themselves.

After a lot of inquiries from acquaintances and people on the street, we decided to take the train to the town of Bludenz by the southern Austrian border. Following various incidents, we found a guide who could take us and some others through the mountains into Switzerland. From there we hoped to arrange passage to New York City where I had an aunt and uncle who could sponsor us. We sold a few pieces of the remaining jewelry to hire the guide and get supplies."

Fritz took a deep breath, gripping the sides of his chair to keep from drowning in this memory. Did he really have to do this?

Lili sensing his anguish, jumped in. "The guide

was young and moved our group at a rapid pace. The trail was rough. I tripped and injured my ankle. We couldn't keep up, so we let the group go on without us."

Fritz took over the narrative. "I left your mother to rest off the path in some bushes while I searched for a shortcut the guide had mentioned. I was studying the map when all of a sudden, I looked up and saw a Russian soldier on the trail in front of me, his gun pointing at my heart."

Larry pushed forward on his chair, totally attentive. Marta's face was chalk-white, panic in her eyes. Did she know what was coming?

"Your mom heard our voices and moved to a brushy area overlooking the trail. Thinking fast, she shoved a huge rock towards us, hitting the soldier and knocking him down. He dropped the gun." Fritz stopped. Beads of sweat poured down his face. His heart thumped with so much violence, he was sure everyone in the room could hear it.

"What happened next, Dad?" Larry whispered.

Fritz took a deep breath and locked his eyes on Lili's. "I took the gun. I shot him. He died."

For a moment no one moved a muscle or took a breath. Then sobs shook Fritz's body. The scene was as stark and vivid right now as it had been 20 years ago. He had extinguished someone else's life. Forever.

Everyone besides Fritz seemed frozen for eternity,

the shocked anguish filling every crack of the room.

"Dad," Marta whispered, stepping into her father's torment, tears sliding down her cheeks, "you didn't have a choice." As Fritz met her eyes, Marta left the chair, throwing her arms around him. Lili immediately joined the embrace and then even Larry did.

Fritz melted into the tears and the hugs. His family knew. And they still loved him. It was a long road ahead, but they could proceed together.

Well-done

Being alone in the quiet car calmed Vivien's jangled nerves. Even after three years, these monthly counselling sessions could set off anxiety bells.

Entering Janelle's office, Vivien startled at the sight of the cupcake and lit candle on the desk.

"This is your graduation celebration," Janelle announced. "You can blow out the candle and congratulate yourself on a journey well-done."

Vivien blushed and blew out the candle. "I don't feel like I am done. There are so many unanswered questions."

"Those questions may always be unanswered. But you have done the difficult work of accepting your past and most importantly, forgiving those who have caused your pain. Think back over all our many weeks together and what has transpired in our conversations. I have to run down the hall to pick up a pamphlet."

Vivien's thoughts flitted back over the litany of sorrows:

Being separated from her family and then learning of her mother and brother's death. She never said good-bye. She never stopped missing them. She never had a mother.

The short reunion with her father ending with his unexplained disappearance. What happened to him? Could he still be alive somewhere? Should she still be trying to find him?

Getting dropped off at the orphanage in Switzerland. A child in a crowd of children. Not knowing the language or what was going to happen to her.

The shuffling from one foster home to another so rapidly that she never got attached to the overworked foster parents, the often cruel foster siblings. Dreaming of the forever home.

The last placement and the horrible, continual abuse that ended her childhood innocence.

Even the sponsored trip to America – a generous gift for a young, frightened 18 year old, faltering in the English language and masquerading as an independent adult.

Through it all, something, someone had carried her and guided her and allowed her to live an emotionally healthy life.

As Janelle sat back down in patient silence, Vivien drew in a deep breath. "I am so thankful for your help. And Annie's too. I could never have figured any of this out alone."

Janelle grinned. "Eat a cupcake, and move forward in confidence. We are both still around if needed."

To the Park

Marta tossed the head of lettuce into the shopping cart. What else was on the list? Scrutinizing her mom's miniscule cursive, she almost bumped into the woman in front of her.

"Excuse me," Marta said as the woman turned around. "Oh wow, Mrs. Harris!"

"Marta? My goodness, I almost didn't recognize you. You have certainly grown up. I bet you are graduating soon."

"Yes. Next month," Marta answered. "I'm sorry you never came back to our high school. You were my favorite teacher."

Vivien smiled, "I've missed teaching, but I had a new baby last year, so I've had my hands full. In fact, I'm meeting my husband and children at Lincoln Park, right around the corner in a few minutes. Can you join us for a little chat?"

Marta glanced at her watch. "Sure. I'm not due

home for a while. It would be great to meet your family."

*****

Vivien pulled into the park entrance. Paul was already pushing the children on the swings, accompanied by their delighted screams. The sun felt warm for mid-April and highlighted a few brave buds poking up through dry leaves.

Marta parked next to her, and together they headed across the grass to the playground. "How about college?" Vivien asked.

"I am going to the University of Massachusetts. They accepted me into the Honors Program."

Vivien patted her on the back. "Wonderful! Will you major in writing?"

Marta shook her head. "I haven't enjoyed writing as much since I left your class. I am thinking of becoming a social worker. I want to do something to help people."

"That's a terrific choice. You have such a compassionate, tender heart."

Paul waved as they approached the swings. "Marta, this is my husband, Paul. The little girl is Karin." Marta shook Paul's hand and grinned at the blonde, blue-eyed, miniature version of Vivien. "And that chunky toddler with the filthy face is Peter."

Karin yelled, "Mommy, push me higher." Vivien

obliged as Karin giggled with delight. "I am three, and my name has an 'i'," Karin informed Marta with a proud smile.

"Three is so big," Marta nodded, chuckling at the little girl. "And I like your name with an 'i'."

"They are both named after my parents," Vivien said, "which reminds me – we never did finish our stories." This sun-drenched day could be the perfect setting for that closure, she thought, adjusted superficially for the audience and circumstances.

"Daddy, let's go to the sides," Karin shrieked. Vivien nodded in agreement and Paul followed the children to the other side of the playground.

Vivien knew this conversation could be uncomfortable for them, but she felt like she owed it to Marta to finish what they both had started.

"I already told you about our trek through the mountains. I never did find out what happened to my father. When he disappeared he was wearing a Russian soldier's uniform. I always wondered if maybe he ran into another escaping Nazi who thought he was the enemy. I miss my family every day, but I have learned to accept all the unknowns and be grateful for my life now. What about the rest of your family's story?"

Marta took a deep breath and plunged into the narrative of her parents' journey after the War through the mountains, towards freedom in Switzerland. When she got to the encounter between her father and the Russian soldier, the words started sticking in her throat. For these last few weeks, the graphic images of her gentle dad's violent confrontation haunted her waking and sleeping moments.

Focusing on the grass at her feet, Marta gulped. "He picked up the gun and shot the soldier."

Vivien's sharp gasp was like a sword thrust. Her face was ashy pale. Eyes gripped with horror. Body quivering. Mind screamed. Was it possible? There were so many intersecting details. Was it only a coincidence?

Compelled, she forced a reply, voice quaking, "I think that soldier could have been my father."

A cold silence all of a sudden hung starkly between them in sharp contrast to the warm sun and joyful playground sounds.

Marta's mind and heart were encased in icy disbelief. She never could have imagined this. Or invented it. What could she do?

"I don't know what to say," Marta choked out. "I am so sorry. So very sorry."

Dinner and More Truth

After dumping the whole story out to Paul that night, it took Vivien several days to process the pain and then ask for help. She set up a meeting with Janelle, asking if Annie could be invited also.

"I didn't want to repeat this saga twice, and since you guys are the original colleagues, I figured we could all three sift through this together."

As she retold Marta's story, Vivien watched their faces shift from curiosity to incredulous dismay. "Now I have some closure to my chronicle, but how on earth do I proceed?"

Annie spoke up first. "What's the biggest lesson you have learned the last few years?"

"Without a doubt – it's forgiveness," Vivien said. "Thanks to you two I have embraced the truth that God forgave me, and because of that, I can forgive others."

"Even such a tragic event as this?" Janelle probed.

Vivien paused. She had been wrestling with that the last two days even though she knew the answer. "Yes."

"Why don't you set up a dinner meeting with Marta and her family? One of us can facilitate the conversation," Annie offered.

"OK. I'll let the two of you fight it out for that privilege. It won't be easy, but I do see the necessity," Vivien said.

"How about if Annie goes? Having an "official" therapist present might seem too unnatural," Janelle answered.

*****

A week later Lili hung up the phone. "Your Mrs. Harris just invited us all to dinner at her house tomorrow."

Marta's shock was mirrored in both her parents' faces. They had discussed the surprise ending over and over this last week. This invitation sounded like they would be all reliving the painful, awkward nightmare.

Nevertheless, two days later, Marta and her parents stood at the door of the Harris's trim Colonial house, her dad clutching an enormous mixed bouquet of spring flowers. Larry had a tennis game which couldn't be missed, to his huge relief, they all knew.

Paul answered the bell and invited them in. The living room was cozy with overstuffed furniture, wood crackling in the fireplace, toys scattered on the shag carpet. Vivien introduced them to Annie. With eager excitement, Karin and Peter displayed their favorite trucks, books, and dolls, keeping the mood light - and the elephant in the closet. For now.

Roast chicken, *späetzle*, and cucumber salad focused everyone's attention on eating, complimenting Vivien, and reminiscing about the German food that Austrians also enjoyed.

After plenty of small talk while consuming with relish the chocolate *sachertorte* and hazelnut ice cream,

Paul announced he would put the children to bed. Everyone else helped Vivien clear the table and rinse the dishes. And then there was nothing left to distract them as they headed back to the living room.

Vivien cleared her throat. "There is no easy way to do this, so I'm going to dive right in. Both our families have been horribly affected by the events occurring during World War II. My father was a Nazi officer, part of the army and movement that murdered many people in your family and millions of Jews in the western world. Marta and I discovered that through an unfortunate accident, Fritz, you encountered my dad on that mountain path outside of Bludenz. You shot and killed my father."

The room was soundless. No one moved a muscle. What was the response to such stark truth?

After hushed seconds stretched to minutes, Fritz rose from his chair, sinking to his knees before Vivien. "Your father's death has tormented me for all these years. To now meet his orphaned daughter and glimpse his humanness makes it even more heinous. Yes, he was part of a murderous machine, but he was a somebody, a husband, a father, and a soldier, obeying orders. I have no words to adequately express my anguish. I don't even have the right to ask your forgiveness.

In answer, Vivien took Fritz's trembling fingers and squeezed them. "I hold no grudges. Several years ago I realized my life was not in my hands but in my heavenly Father's instead. Since then, He has given me a new life, a new faith, a new family, and a new chance for happiness. And because I have been forgiven much, I am able to forgive you. I know it must be hard to believe, but from the bottom of my heart, please accept that."

Fritz nodded wordlessly and engulfed Vivien with both arms. Lili and Marta joined them. Somehow they all ended up on the floor in a gigantic huddle of hugs and tears.

The silence was long and comfortable now, uniting them in a bond of sorrow, compassion, and the very beginning of understanding. From the living room window, the moon was peering from behind clouds. A full moon. A new family unit, full of mercy. And more chapters to write for those yet to come who will need to know.

*****

December 2023

Kalispell, Montana

Marta toured the house one last time. Piles of presents surrounded the tree. The table was festively set with her favorite holiday porcelain. The traditional Sauerbraten simmered in the oven, filling the house with aromas of marinated onions and carrots. She sank into her rocker, relishing the last minutes of silence before the rest of the family returned from skiing.

From the guestroom, Susie cooed that she was awake, standing in her crib, arms raised, eyes sparkling, waiting to be picked up. Marta carried her to the rocker. Snuggling with this toddler only worked if she was somewhat sleepy. And how sweet it was! Grandchildren were indeed the icing on the cake of life.

Her parents would have loved being great-grandparents. Marta missed them acutely. Who they were and what they had done impacted her each day, along with regrets for not appreciating her mom more and recognizing her quiet strength. And all those questions that could never now be answered.

Marta rocked the contented girl who was mesmerized by the sparkling tree and the heirloom ornament spinning in slow motion, revealing each of its facets. So many episodes of her 72 years rotated along with it—her childhood in Elmsburg and the decadent, wandering, searching years in Oregon which led to the miracles which transformed her along the way to the woman, mother, and grandmother she was today.

On the treetop, the Star of Bethlehem twinkled at her. "Did you really want to know?" she imagined the star asking.

"Yes," Marta whispered. "Thank you, God, for telling me. And for making me part of Your story."

*****

Acknowledgements

I could not have taken this journey alone.

My parents documented their lives in their autobiographies that contained many details which I incorporated into this novel. More importantly, the way they lived spoke volumes to those of us watching. I am so grateful for their long lives and all the love and wisdom of our heritage they shared with me and my family.

Thank you to my sister, Judie, who has walked with me through all these years and this process of writing, as well as to Kathy Watters and Linda Kuntz who edited my early attempts.

One of the best things about writing is being involved in the writing community. I am very grateful to my critique group – Karen Wills, Carmen Alexander, and especially Janice Goodison and Bonnie Smith for their amazing feedback and help.

Most of all I am grateful for Jesus Christ who designed this journey and provides the forgiveness, hope, and strength we need to travel on it.